PENGUIN BOOKS

THE BOOK OF HOPE: EXTRAORDINARY STORIES OF ORDINARY INDIANS

In 1609, the world's first newspaper, arguably, was published in Strausbourg. It was aptly named Relation aller Fürnemmen und gedenckwürdigen Historien—which translates into Account of all distinguished and commendable stories. Unfortunately, over the next 400 years, news media has mutated into an unrecognizable form far removed from its original DNA—to become sensationalist, scandalous, and downright polarizing.

It was this vicious cycle that The Better India sought to break. It was the first to show the world that solutions based stories are equally important in a world that is obsessed with sensationalism.

The endeavour of The Better India is to shine the light on the positive, the good, the kind, and thereby restoring the faith of humanity in the humanity of humans.

The Better India is the world's largest platform that uses the power of stories to drive large-scale social and economic change.

T0002178

The Book of Hope

Extraordinary STORIES OF ordinary INDIANS

PENGUIN BOOKS

An imprint of Penguin Random House

PENGUIN BOOKS

USA | Canada | UK | Ireland | Australia
New Zealand | India | South Africa | China

Penguin Books is part of the Penguin Random House group of companies
whose addresses can be found at global.penguinrandomhouse.com

Published by Penguin Random House India Pvt. Ltd
4th Floor, Capital Tower 1, MG Road,
Gurugram 122 002, Haryana, India

First published in Penguin Books by Penguin Random House India 2021

ISBN 9780143454182

Typeset in Minion Pro by Manipal Technologies Limited, Manipal
Printed at Thomson Press India Ltd, New Delhi

www.penguin.co.in

Dedicated to the changemaker in you

Contents

Section III
Finding Hope

Section IV
On Loss

Section V
All It Takes is One Person

Section VI
Business With a Heart

Foreword

If a man from Mars landed on Earth today and picked up a newspaper or heard a news broadcast, he would probably turn tail and head straight back to where he came from. Going by the headlines alone, Earth often appears to be a place that is in a constant state of tension, confrontation, selfishness, and greed. In this age of instant communication, it's the bad news that travels fastest and furthest, because it's easier to focus on the bad than to look for the good. This relentless onslaught of negativity unleashes a pandemic of distrust and anxiety and despair.

I believe, however, that human beings are inherently good, and they never give up the quest for happy endings. That is why stories end with 'happily ever after'. That is why the good guy in the movies wins against all odds. That is why history shows us again and again that the good ultimately triumphs.

The pandemic has taught me that not all heroes come out of the pages of a Marvel comic, and fly around with capes or in a Batmobile. Some of them wield a stethoscope. Some of them wield a broom. Some of them deliver essential groceries to our doorsteps. And even in normal times many of them educate children, many of them feed the needy, many of them save trees, many of them invent low-cost devices for households and the handicapped. The world, in general, and India, in particular, is full of these unsung heroes and all of them have a superpower. Their superpower is that they see a problem and they want to be a part of the solution.

Their stories need to be told. And the good news that they bring needs to be disseminated far and wide. That is why it was a joy for me to discover The Better India, with its mission to shine a light on the good, rather than on scandal and sensation. By going against the grain and holding firm for over a decade now, The Better India has shown that positive and inspiring coverage has a significant place in our day-to-day lives and can reignite our belief that our country is full of people who want to impact their world and make it better. Their heroes are everyday people who dare to believe, who dare to trust, who dare to dream, and who dare to do what is right. These heroes come from all corners of the country, and by amplifying their deeds through the power of social media, The Better India amplifies their impact ten-fold. In the course of this, they are also mapping the march of change across the country.

I have discovered this myself through platforms like Twitter, where I often find (and share) moments of outside-of-the-box thinking that are significant because they light a candle, rather than curse the darkness. These are the moments and stories that need to be highlighted more than ever—because they have the power to change the world for good.

People talk about reimagining the future—but I believe that a better future is already here. All that's required is for its voice to be heard and magnified. Thank you, The Better India, for doing that so well.

Anand G. Mahindra

Introduction

What can a good story do?

A good story can connect a photography club for the blind with a visually impaired girl who always dreamed of becoming a photographer—so she can finally realize her dream.

A good story can be one that connects a school for underprivileged children in Chennai needing repairs with a team of engineers in Bangalore with the intent to help—so that their broken wall can be rebuilt.

A good story can also help a social entrepreneur on the brink of bankruptcy meet an impact investor seeking to scale up sustainable innovations—so that his amazing product gets a new lease of life.

These are just three from among thousands of good stories in The Better India that have had a positive impact on individuals, society, policies, and the environment.

So how did it all begin? On a rainy morning in July 2008, while sipping on the morning tea and reading the daily newspaper, we both asked ourselves a question—'What is the use of this news?' Sure, it helps highlight the issues plaguing our country, creates some furore and brings in a resignation or two, makes us all angry at the system—but at the end of it all, what does it really achieve? Does it inspire us to action or paralyze us with demotivation? Does it help us see how we can solve things for the better or make us believe that nothing will ever change? And most importantly, does it give us hope or throw us deeper into the throes of despair?

With all these questions floating in front of our eyes, the chai was quickly forgotten, and we scanned the newspapers carefully to find news that we could use. News and stories that made us more aware, more enabled, or more empowered to do our part. But alas, these seemed to be prominently absent. We went online and scanned all Indian websites to find no hope. This suddenly made us more aware of the reason behind the brain drain that we had witnessed first-hand—most of our friends had left the country in search of greener pastures abroad, believing that things were never going to improve here.

Strangely, we did not see the glass half empty. We saw dozens of people we knew working in their own little ways to make a difference. We met inspiring personalities who selflessly devoted their lives to the improvement of the downtrodden. We came across organizations and institutions struggling to stay afloat but working hard to achieve their purpose. And we felt that all that focus on negative and sensational news was not fair to them.

That's when The Better India was born. What started as an idea of harnessing the power of stories to inspire change became a movement of positive impact where thousands of volunteers reached out to us to contribute news from the farthest reaches of the country and from the most diverse areas of work.

When we launched 'formally', we thought we had turned some corner. Little did we know that it was merely the opening step of an enormous journey that would consume us entirely. The corners came and were turned, in quick succession after that.

Our first employee was paid monthly via cheques from our savings account. Our first office, a co-working space, after working out of cafes and from our homes for years. Our first million page views in one year, then in one month, then in one week, and then a million views a day. Our first 'big impact' moment came when we helped set up sustainable enterprises for the widows of farmers who had committed suicide in rural, arid Maharashtra.

We learned hard lessons and turned them around as well. The difference between doing something and doing the right thing, between those who collect funds and those who use them, between the talkers and doers. At all times, we kept clear of politics and religion, keeping our focus on the unsung everyday heroes. They worked silently on the ground, transforming lives without seeking publicity, often making huge sacrifices so someone else may have a chance to live with dignity.

We grew—first by a little and then by leaps and bounds. We found investors who believed in us and brands who wanted to support change and progress along with us. And we found cause after cause whose noble aims pushed us to grow even further.

We had begun this because the mainstream did not exist where we wanted them to be. Today, we are our own broad stream, with almost every media outlet building its own 'good news' sections, often directly inspired by our journey. Our articles are read by tens of millions, and hundreds of millions more reach us through social media or our videos. And not a day goes by without someone reaching out to us, telling us how our work made a difference in their lives. After twelve years, we can safely say—the good news is here to stay.

Today, a good story has become so many things. It has a place among the important coverage the rest of the media does. It shines a spotlight on those doing good. It implies that their efforts—helping trigger real, on-ground impact—are being acknowledged and loved by our readers. It is read by millions, who now consider reading about something good a natural part of their daily lives, perhaps even with their morning tea.

So, what else can a good story be? It can also be a book; one you can hold and treasure and be inspired by, at those times when you feel what we felt all those years ago: 'Is everything in this country really all that bad?'

While COVID ravaged the world, it also brought out the need to find hope, compassion, courage, and resilience like never before. In the extreme darkness, we searched for the beacons of light that shone through and guided our way—extraordinary Indians who never gave up, those who provided relief to helpless communities, selfless frontline workers who went the extra mile to serve the society, incredible teachers who went door-to-door just so that no underprivileged kid got left behind, those who fed the hungry and the homeless, and so many more.

This book is one more reason to believe in our country and the 1.3 billion people who inhabit it. We hope this book shows you that India is much, much better than you think.

Anuradha Kedia and Dhimant Parekh

Section I

Love Always Finds a Way

*'Most people need love and acceptance
a lot more than they need advice.'*

Bob Goff.

'What's Not to Love in This Life?'

Vidya Raja

Yogendra Shankar Chaudhry (eighty-seven) and Lata Chaudhry (eighty-four), residents of Mumbai, were married for fifty-three years before life as they knew it changed completely. After a series of minor incidents, Lata was diagnosed with Alzheimer's four years ago. What should have been a peaceful existence in their eighties was shaken up by the diagnosis and the subsequent changes it brought.

Lata's diagnosis impacted not just Yogendra, but also their son, Paresh, and their immediate family and friends who have been in constant contact with them.

While there are more than 4 million Indians suffering from some form of dementia, what's unique about Lata's story is how her primary caregiver and the love of her life, Yogendra, has helped her revisit a passion she nurtured as a young girl of eleven. Warli paintings, a tribal artform, has her lost for hours on a single piece. The walls in their Bandra home are covered with her vibrant artwork.

'She is trying her best,' said Yogendra. The exhaustion is palpable in his tone.

He adds, 'She forgets things very easily—one moment she said something and then a few seconds later she has no recollection of what she said. These are difficult times but she is my wife and of course, I will support her.'

Paresh, their son, who comes by every day to have lunch with his parents, said, 'Poised and always in-control—that is how I remember amma. She was never one to be fazed by any situation. Even now, there is that glint in her eyes that I see every once in a while.'

While they have help at home, Yogendra takes special care of Lata. But over the last few years, it has taken a toll on his health.

Memories of a different life

In the early 1950s, Yogendra had moved to Mumbai from Uttar Pradesh in pursuit of his dream of joining Bollywood. It was during this stint that he stayed as a paying guest (PG) in Lata's home and that is how the two first met. Recalling those moments, Yogendra said, 'I don't know about love at first sight but there was mutual liking—not just with Lata but also her family.'

He blushes when he said, 'We got married in a small ceremony at the Mahalaxmi temple in Mumbai. It was a union that was blessed by all.'

He adds, 'Her family was happy to have one of their daughters married off.'

Lata on the other hand was born and raised in Mumbai and belonged to a very well-respected family. Her father, Rambhau Tatnis was a noted journalist, editor and publisher of one of India's first pre-Independence Marathi newspapers— *Vividhvritta*.

Lata attended the Ram Mohan English school in Girgaon and since her early years, she had displayed a keen interest in music and art. She also holds the distinction of performing with Usha Mangeshkar, Asha Bhonsle's and Lata Mangeshkar's sister. Lata was also good at painting and would often display her canvas artwork at school exhibitions.

Even though she was not trained to be an artist, she had a natural flair for it. However, her life turned upside down when her father passed away. The situation at home changed dramatically and Lata had to drop out of college to help support the family. Here again, she turned to art and started selling her paintings and some hand-painted saris.

It is no surprise then that with her life-altering diagnosis four years ago, the only thing that Lata seemed to remember very well was her love for art and the time she had spent in her father's home.

However, today, her memories haven't faded but her present seems hazy. 'She often asks about her mother and siblings. When I explain to her that they have all passed away, she gets upset. She asks me how it is possible for all of them to have died,' said Paresh.

Yogendra interjects here to share that one of the reasons why he became a paying guest at Lata's home was because they needed the money and letting out a few rooms in the house meant additional income for the family.

While Yogendra came to Mumbai to become an actor he chose to marry Lata and also took up a job at Siemens. 'Lata politely asked me to choose between marrying her and Bollywood, and of course, without an iota of doubt in my head, I chose her,' he said.

A Fragile Mind

One of the proudest artistic moments in Lata's life was when she painted a sari for a school competition and yesteryear actor, Durga Khote, was called as the judge. 'Shocked with the talent reflected in my work, she promptly asked me how old I was. I said, "Aunty, talent has no age!" in a matter-of-fact manner,' said Lata, mentioning that she won first prize at the competition.

She may often forget if she has eaten or if she has showered in the morning, but when she holds her brush and starts painting, she is transported to a different world. Lata can spend hours on her art and enjoys the Warli art form a great deal. The walls in their Bandra home are all adorned with Lata's artwork. 'She is the most peaceful when she is painting—it's what she knows the best,' said Paresh.

She used sketching and painting as a coping mechanism after her father's passing. 'I always had the sensibility of using colour and used to advise my elder sister's art students on colour combinations,' Lata reminisces.

Today, the only thing that has remained constant for Lata is Yogendra's unflinching support. Paresh said, 'We all talk about amma's diagnosis but papa also has it tough. Being the primary caregiver is not easy and he's not getting any younger either.' From being Lata's biggest cheerleader to patiently answering all her questions, Yogendra refuses to give up on her. Despite Paresh living in the same city, he said that from a familiarity point of view, his mother is most comfortable in their home in Bandra where she has spent more than five decades. 'She refuses to move out of this home,' adds Paresh.

There have been moments of utter chaos and fear as well in the last four years, like the time when Lata accidently left the house. Recalling the incident Paresh said, 'Papa was taking his afternoon nap when amma left the house without informing him. I remember my father being very distraught when he said he couldn't find amma. It turned out that there was a death in the neighbourhood and she had gone to meet the family. Without thinking too much she had gone along with the family to the crematorium too. Once there, she had forgotten how she got there and what she should do to get back. Thankfully, we found her safe and sound . . . but that fear was something else.'

Lata's mind has taken her back to the late 1940s, as she often talks about their old driver, Pandu, who spent considerable time with the family. She also lists the various cars that the family owned at the time: 'We had Peugeot, Plymouth, Lincoln, Chevrolet, Ford, and so many more cars.'

Despite knowing that she isn't quite herself these days, Lata refuses to get help and insists on cooking three meals even today. 'Self-reliance—this is the value that amma instilled in us when we were growing up and she continues to practise it even today when her mental faculties seem to be failing her. Even now, she wakes up every single morning brimming with optimism,' said Paresh. Hearing this, Lata adds, 'What's not to love in this life?'

Letting Love Bloom, Organically

Lekshmi Priya S.

Everyone wants their wedding to be unique and unforgettable. But in India, people go out of their way to ensure that their special day remains indeed special. For some, it is a display of grandeur and extravaganza, while for others the day is earmarked to send out a message.

We have all been part of one or the other, but have you ever attended a marriage ceremony where everything that was served in the wedding banquet was cultivated and harvested by the bride and the groom?

A farming couple from Kerala did exactly that. Love for agriculture was what brought the destinies of Vani and Vijith together, and over a decade ago, they decided to start their married life as an ode to that shared passion.

A native of Haripad town of Alappuzha district, Vani always nursed an affinity for agriculture, and she even fought with her parents to opt for a degree in agriculture, despite showing an aptitude for a promising future in medicine. On the other hand, Vijith wasn't as clear-headed about his future plans. Unsure about which career path to follow, he buckled under family pressure and took up engineering.

However, one thing that really interested Vijith, right from his school days, was nature and he would sign up for every environment camp that came along his way. This devoted participation became even more pronounced during his college days. Along with many of his friends, Vijith would take part in several plantation drives.

'I'd like to attribute my passion for the environment to two significant people in my life—late Shiva Prasad Sir and Mohan Kumar Sir. Known eco-warriors in Kerala, both were teachers who would often be part of these camps. It was their knowledge and expertise that has made me the environmentally-conscious person that I am today," said Vijith.

It was during one of these camps that Vijith and Vani met for the first time, and remained in touch for a very interesting reason.

'Perhaps it was instilled in me during the random plantation drives, but I had this habit of collecting seeds and nurturing saplings, mostly native species like *njaval* (jamun) and *elanji* (Bullet wood tree). I'd supply these to anyone who'd ask me. My friends also helped me out in this pursuit. Because of this habit, Vani would reach out to me for different saplings,' said Vijith.

By then, Vani had completed her BSc in agriculture, and was working with the Watershed Department in Thrissur, while Vijith was employed as a Sub-Station Operator with the Electricity Board in Athani.

In the meantime, they would keep meeting during various environment camps and their friendship cemented further.

Seeing the passion that Vani harboured for agriculture, even Vijith's interest peaked and they decided to together pursue MSc in ecology and environmental sciences from Pondicherry University.

'Unfortunately, Vani's father fell ill after we had joined the course, and she had to drop out to take care of her parents and grandmother. Unlike my personal interest in plants and farming, Vani hails from a family that used to farm quite actively, and grew many types of vegetables and edible tubers. Everyone in her family had good knowledge on not just farming but also on gardening as well as ayurvedic plants. To sustain the family, she decided to start farming across her ancestral land in Haripad,' recalls Vijith.

And joining Vani in this pursuit was Vijith, who also left the course soon.

Together with a few friends, they started work over a 4.5-acre plot. Vijith credits Vani of being the major guiding force, whose vision, knowledge, and experience helped him learn and understand the ways of farming more intensively.

'For me, it was the beginning of a life dedicated towards farming and along with that, biodiversity conservation. This plot was sparsely vegetated so we decided to do what we've done since our college days—plant trees and saplings!' he said.

Somewhere along this time, Vani popped the question to Vijith. 'She has always been focused that way. All these years that we have been together, both as friends and as spouses, she has been clear-headed about what she wanted and also better at decision-making. Though I'd always liked her, I never gave a serious thought to getting married until she proposed!' laughs Vijith.

Along with marriage, she'd also proposed the idea of growing everything they'd need to prepare the wedding feast, which Vijith readily agreed to. 'Perhaps it is possible today that people might want to do something this unique, but ten years ago, it was unheard of. Our whole family wholeheartedly supported us to turn our wish into a reality,' he adds.

And thus began a full-fledged journey into the agrarian world—this time, hand in hand.

But the duo was adamant about one thing. Whatever they grew should be organic and kind to the environment instead of damaging it. An important aspect for Vijith and Vani here was to steer clear of agricultural politics.

'By agricultural politics, I mean how our native crop species have diminished and perhaps even gone forever, thanks to the prevalence of genetically engineered and hybrid seeds. We wanted to bring back different indigenous varieties of crops and cultivate those, as they were better habituated to our region and resistant to diseases. Soil quality as well as groundwater table remain in check, unlike the hybrid seeds which overmine all the resources and leave the soil unfit for use after a few cycles. This led us to collect and preserve native seed varieties of perhaps every vegetable, fruit, and herb variety that we have come across so far,' explains Vijith.

Different varieties of beans, ladies finger, *chena* (elephant foot yam), *chembu* (colocasia), *kachil* (greater yam), brinjal, plantain, mango—they have tried their hand at almost everything.

Furthermore, their relentless tree plantation endeavours have resulted in the creation of a self-sustaining farmland that has over 5000 trees and plants. Some patches have been let alone to develop like *kaavu* (an ancient practice in Kerala under which forest fragments were given sacred and religious connotations and left untouched by local communities). Alongside, there are also ten ponds spread across their land, of which some already existed and the rest were created by the couple and their friends in time.

Using only organic and home prepared manure and compost for the crops, the couple sold their produce outside their home during the initial days.

'When the production started increasing beyond what our friends and neighbours could buy from us, we thought of opening a shop. Things worked in our favour, when a nearby tailoring shop closed down and we took over. My sister and mother helped in revamping the store through their artwork, and we also have a vertical garden set up here. Because it is possible that we may not have enough farm produce for sale round the year, we have teamed up with other organic farmers who would like to sell through our store, Prakrithi Jaiva Kalavara. Alongside, we also sell value-added products made from organic crops like dried plantain and beans,' Vijith adds.

A rather interesting practice that the couple has maintained from the start, despite opening their store, is allowing people to pluck the produce of their choice straight from the fields.

In their pursuit of making their living space entirely sustainable, their farmland has three biogas plants. Compost is generated from these plants in just a day and even their toilet is linked to one of them. They also source food waste from nearby hotels, which can be used as compost after being treated in the plants. In addition to all of this, the couple has installed a solar power plant in the farm that supplies enough electricity to power their house throughout the night.

Their farm is open to everyone who is interested in nature and farming and Vijith and Vani have been particularly keen on hosting kids. 'Initially, kids from nearby areas would come by and spend the entire day here. We would also organize day nature camps. Seeing that these kids loved being here and even showed an inclination to stay back, we were motivated to host proper camps for kids with varied activities and thus, Mango Showers Camp came to being,' Vijith said.

With the first edition of Mango Showers getting a fantastic response from kids and their parents, Vijith is quite hopeful that children of the future will become more environmentally-conscious, and cultivate an interest in agriculture as well.

While Vijith has been taking care of the farm, Vani is currently in Thiruvananthapuram, preparing for the UPSC exams. 'She felt that there were a lot of necessary changes that needed to come in the existing system. As simple farmers, it is not possible [to bring change], but if we are part of the system, there is still some hope. Even I had dedicated an entire year for the same but buckled down later. But she is determined and is putting her heart and soul in the pursuit,' Vijith proudly adds.

For the future, Vijith shares that they have demarcated three patches in the farm to nurture fruit forests. 'We plan on kickstarting the plantation by the end of May, keeping the onset of monsoon in mind,' he concludes.

Middle-Class and Gay

Rinchen Norbu Wangchuk

The Supreme Court verdict on Section 377 of the Indian Penal Code gave the LGBT community in India a lot of hope.

Justice DY Chandrachud said that a person's choice of a partner is a fundamental right, and it can include a same-sex partner. 'Our focus is not only on the sexual act but the relationship between two consenting adults and the manifestation of their rights under Articles 14 and 21 . . . we are dwelling on the nature of (the) relationship and not marriage . . . we want the relationship to be protected under fundamental rights and not to suffer moral policing,' he said while delivering the landmark ruling in September 2018.

For thirty-two-year-old Kaushik, a materials engineer working at a Paris-based company, the proceedings in the Supreme Court have given him a lot of hope.

'I am happy to see that the discussions in court are going beyond just the question of the sexual act being decriminalized and that questions of discrimination are openly discussed for all branches of sexual orientation. But fingers crossed till it is done,' he said.

Born and brought up in Bengaluru to a middle-class Tamil Brahmin family, Kaushik grew up like any other boy from the same social milieu. His father was working as an officer at a bank, while his mother tended to affairs at home.

After studying in a reputed South Bengaluru school, he joined the prestigious Indian Institute of Technology Madras (IIT-M). He studied metallurgy and materials engineering there and then decided to pursue his PhD in Switzerland.

This is the middle-class Indian dream personified. But it wasn't all smooth sailing.

Kaushik was just twelve when he became first aware of his attraction to men. Thankfully, for boys like him, the internet helped him access the 'secret world' of anonymous chat rooms, where there were others like him, including those from India.

'For that split second, in a crowded internet café (we did not have a computer at home till late), you felt a little less alone,' he said.

He did suffer bullying in school every now and then, but it 'had to do with me not being loud and brash enough to reply to those who charged at me,' he said.

Nonetheless, the attraction to men only grew stronger with age. But the lack of any visibility for the LGBT community back then made him think that it was just a 'phase' and that it would all be 'normal'. Kaushik believed then that he would eventually 'grow up', marry, and have children.

'Also, in a society that deflates sexuality so hard, it is difficult in such times to differentiate an intimate camaraderie towards people of the other sex with love. So, for a long time, I believed I was bisexual, for a long time before I could finally accept my orientation,' he said.

Things, however, began to change for Kaushik when he got into IIT-Madras. 'IIT was a completely new start for me, and I decided to take on the occasional bullying with confidence, which changed everything. I managed to make a lot of friends and I didn't care about rumours that were spread about me. That confidence has only stayed with me, thankfully,' he said.

Having said that, there were barriers that stood before Kaushik from realizing his sexual identity in IIT, thanks to homophobia that once pervaded the student community.

'I could say that I was ignorant too,' he said with a smile. However, all that changed when he moved to Switzerland for his PhD.

In an evidently more open society, the process of exploring one's sexual identity gets a lot easier. However, the turning point for him was meeting his now-husband Glenn, a human rights advocate in Geneva, who possesses a special liking for Bangalore masala dosas, puliyogare and rava kesari!

'He wore his sexual orientation with so much ease that I started seeing myself as capable of having the same kind of confidence. With time, this confidence grew, and like most other gay folks, the first person I came out to was myself. The moment I could tell myself without hesitation that I was gay was a moment of such relief. There was suddenly so much more hope, and it just felt right saying it. I had come around to accepting my identity fully, and it just fed into the self-confidence. Once that set in, coming out to friends was much easier,' he said.

The next step was coming out to his parents in the same year, 2012.

'I knew in the back of my mind that they would be all right with it, but the question that I asked myself was for how long? When I did tell them, they were surprisingly open about it. My parents may not be very highly educated. But they are intelligent enough to not rely on clichés to feed into their fears. They were curious to understand the life I was living and what I was feeling,' he said proudly.

A common narrative among queer citizens coming out to their near and dear ones in India is one of pain, separation, trauma, social exclusion and, more often than not, harassment. Kaushik's story is one of love, compassion, curiosity and, more importantly, acceptance.

'My parents were courageous enough to ask me all sort of personal questions. This kind of openness in their generation, and in India in general, is extremely rare and I was fortunate enough to have it. The least I could do was respond to their efforts with honesty. The whole conversation lasted about two hours and at the end of it, they just hugged me and said they accepted me for who I was as long as I was happy,' said Kaushik.

Having said that, Kaushik's parents initially did not envision the possibility of two men falling in love, and there were fears that their son would navigate the world alone. Kaushik put these fears to rest weeks later and told them about Glenn.

'Within a matter of months, they were able to see that I was happy being who I am and with whom I wanted to be. It didn't take them much time to accept my boyfriend as a part of the family. And they still do,' he said.

They tied the knot in December 2015 at Glenn's hometown in France.

Does Kaushik envision the same for queer people living in India? Once the court does scrap Section 377 from the statute books, Kaushik feels that the next step forward is the legitimization of non-heterosexual couples, which offers at least some recognition for their status in society.

'Since many other questions such as live-in relationships are being dealt with, they could be extended to all sorts of couples, providing a much more open social space for sexual minorities. I'm very hopeful for the future of sexual minorities in India. I believe that we live in a society that is rapidly changing. We cannot be the largest democracy and at the same time not recognize these issues,' said Kaushik.

And he's right.

How does he deal with discrimination? Kaushik admits that hearing homophobic slurs once in a while in India does stir up past insecurities. 'So, depending on when and where I face discrimination, I choose to address it or not. In safe spaces and with non-violent people, I would discuss it and see where it comes from and get them to reflect on it. In spaces where I do not feel comfortable, or I feel intimidated by the people using homophobic slurs, I choose not to,' he said.

And finally, does he have a message for young people in India still in the closet or struggling with their sexual identity? 'Coming out is a personal choice, so trust your guts on when and how you want to. At the same time, the internet provides for a lot of safe spaces for discussions. If you have questions, make sure you go to reliable sources to find the answers,' said Kaushik.

It takes real courage of conviction to come out. The process isn't easy, despite what you may have read in Kaushik's story. Fortunately, he was met with love and compassion in large parts.

This may not be the case every time, but Kaushik's story does tell you that such possibilities exist.

'She's the Battery to My Bullet'

Vidya Raja

Think motorbike with a sidecar and the first image that pops into one's mind is of Jai and Veeru from the cult movie *Sholay*. But seventy-seven-year-old Mohanlal P. Chauhan has a different opinion. 'Forget Jai and Veeru. Once you read our story the motorbike with the sidecar will only remind you of us,' he said.

Mohanlal and his wife, the seventy-one-year-old Leelaben, have covered over 30,000 kilometres over four road trips on their 1974 vintage Royal Enfield bike.

The first few solo trips that Mohanlal embarked on were for fun, but he said that he missed Leelaben's company. The desire to travel together led Mohanlal to fix the Bullet with a sidecar.

In 2011, Mohanlal, a former employee of the Oil and Natural Gas Corporation (ONGC), suffered a heart attack after which the doctors forbade him from even climbing stairs.

'Not one to be sitting at home, he decided to live his life on his own terms,' said Leelaben.

After opting for voluntary retirement from ONGC, Mohanlal started going on short solo trips in 2015. 'I remember exploring nearby places with my father on his scooter as a kid. After my retirement, when I started going on trips, I felt almost like I had a new lease on life,' he said.

'In 2010, Leelaben had a fall and fractured her leg which left her in pain and also slightly handicapped. I knew I wanted her to travel with me, but at the same time I wanted to make the ride easy on her. This was what led to the attachment of the sidecar to the Bullet,' Mohanlal adds.

Do Deewane Shaher Mein

The song 'Do Deewane Shaher Mein' from the movie *Gharonda* (1977) beautifully captures the essence of Mohanlal and Leelaben's journey. In 2016, after having the sidecar attached, the couple embarked on their first trip together. Starting from Vadodara in Gujarat, the couple went through Maharashtra, Kerala, Goa, Karnataka, and Tamil Nadu.

While the couple was looking forward to crossing the borders and visiting Sri Lanka, they were able to go only up to Rameshwaram, Tamil Nadu, due to some political tension. 'The sunrise and sunset at Rameshwaram was something else,' said Leelaben, who adds that witnessing this natural phenomenon was an experience she will never forget. While the couple returned to Vadodara after this Bharat darshan, they were already planning their next trip.

Asked about the difficulties of the planning process, Mohanlal said, 'The planning was not the problem; answering questions and allaying fears and doubts that people had was the problem. Many were convinced that we would not last beyond a few hundred kilometres.'

But in February 2018, the couple took a second trip. This time the destination was Thailand. 'On our journey to reach Thailand, we went through Madhya Pradesh, Uttar Pradesh, Jharkhand, Odisha, West Bengal, Assam, and Meghalaya. Unfortunately, when we reached Meghalaya, there were a few landslides on the way and we were advised not to go forward,' he said. The couple regrets not being able to make it to Thailand, but, in the same breath, add that every destination they crossed has left them with memories to last a lifetime.

Not without Their Share of Pitfalls

In 2018, when the couple was passing through Chitrakoot, Madhya Pradesh, Leelaben had a fall and fractured her ankle, for which she had to undergo a surgery. Having to spend close to a fortnight in the hospital, Mohanlal said, 'This lady is made of very strong stuff. She did not let the fall deter her spirit. With a cast on, she got into the sidecar ready to go. Not once did she say she wanted to get back home. She's the second battery to my Bullet.'

Leelaben also prides herself on being the finance manager of the team and said, 'We budget between Rs 3000 to Rs 4000 as our daily expenditure. This includes our food, stay, petrol, and other miscellaneous costs. Thus far we would have spent Rs 2 lakh on each trip."

In 2019, they covered Rajasthan, Punjab, Himachal Pradesh, and went up to Jammu.

'We have covered almost every state in India. Each one is prettier than the other, and even if you asked me to pick my favourite, I wouldn't be able to,' said Mohanlal. While most people feel homesick on trips, Leelaben said that staying at home for too long makes them rather sick.

'We need to be able to travel and explore places. We are not made to stay put in one place,' she adds.

The last trip that the couple took on their Bullet was in early 2020 when they visited Srisailam in Andhra Pradesh. What keeps them going is their simple outlook on life. 'With every stop, I make sure that I reach out to the chef to request for simple food to be made for us. We are vegetarians and other than onions and potatoes, we eat everything,' said Mohanlal.

Mohanlal shares some of the foods that he likes eating and said, 'Paneer paratha, tomato soup, vegetable pulav, masala *bhat*, curd and one full glass of milk is what my diet consists of. No matter where we went—South or North—our food requirements were always taken care of.'

With the world grappling with the COVID-19 pandemic, travel plans for 2021 have been put on hold. But reminiscing about their trips together, Leelaben said, 'He's my husband but when we travel together, he becomes my best friend. I enjoy riding with him.'

'He Tried to Kill Me'

Gopi Karelia

'Abortion is not expensive. I am sure you can afford it against the massive cost you will incur by raising three daughters. If you go ahead with this decision, you can maybe even save your marriage,' said the doctor as if giving life-saving advice. Three-month pregnant Jasbeer Kaur's expressions said it all. She chose not to degrade herself by participating in the conversation any further and left the hospital.

'I felt liberated by facing the most dreaded advice. When I thought about raising girls all by myself, I was not scared. I was happy about shaping three beautiful individuals. I became a single parent during that fifteen-minute ride from the hospital to my parents' house in 1996,' said Jasbeer, who now lives in Rajasthan's 36 BB village, tells The Better India.

Six months later, Jasbeer gave birth to triplets and walked out of an abusive marriage.

Jasbeer was merely twenty-six at the time, in an era when divorce and the birth of a girl-child were severely looked down upon in her community and village.

Braving constant attacks about her failed marriage and unceasing taunts from the community, Jasbeer single-handedly raised all her daughters—Pradeep, Sandeep, and Mandeep.

Forty-nine-year-old Jasbeer has been an auxiliary nurse for the last twenty-one years in a government hospital to support her daughters. Her triplets have completed their post-graduation and are financially independent.

While Mandeep followed her mother's footsteps and became a nurse, Sandeep is a make-up artist and Pradeep is in the hotel management sector.

'All the credit goes to my lion-hearted mother who never imposed any restrictions on us. She aced both the roles of a mother and a father. She never for once, let us feel that something was missing. She is our confidant and best friend,' said Sandeep.

'She is the bravest woman I know and every day she inspires us to do better. She has gone out of her way to help her patients, especially pregnant women in the hospital. The joy and satisfaction of serving someone is what inspired me to go to the hotel industry,' said Pradeep, who is the youngest.

From being married to an alcoholic to tolerating humiliation to save her family from shame and finally her identity, Jasbeer's journey from fear to courage is extraordinary.

'He Tried to Kill Me'

Daughter of a farmer, Jasbeer had a happy childhood. In her district Gurdaspur in Punjab, girls were not allowed to study, let alone take a job. But Jasbeer's parents encouraged her to pursue a BA from a local college.

When she expressed her desire to become a nurse, her parents got her enrolled in a nursing course.

'I have two sisters and one brother but I have never experienced any bias or discrimination. All of us were encouraged to think independently, which was very rare back in the day,' said Jasbeer.

In 1995, a twenty-six-year-old Jasbeer was married and within a few days, she learnt the truth about her husband. Mental and physical harassment became an everyday affair. To save her family's name, she chose to stay and hoped things would improve. A few months into the marriage, she got pregnant. 'There has been not a single day when I did not cry in that house. The last straw was when they illegally found out the gender of my children during an ultrasound. I had two options—abortion or divorce,' she said.

When she refused an abortion, her former husband tried to murder her by pushing her fingers into a live electric socket. That's when she decided to leave. Fortunately, her parents and brother extended unconditional support to her.

'My mother said if she could raise daughters, then even I could do it. Even though I was aware that eventually, the burden would fall on me, I was happy to know my family had my back. They gave me the strength to fight and build a new life for my unborn babies.' Six months later, Jasbeer delivered three girls, 'They are the best thing that happened to me. I derived energy and strength just by holding them together. I knew life was going to get better,' she recalls.

Building A New Life for Jasbeer

Jasbeer moved to 36 BB village in Padampur district, Rajasthan when the girls were less than a year old. There, she took up the job of the Auxiliary Nurse Midwife in a government hospital.

Besides getting away from her oppressive community and starting afresh, Jasbeer chose the uniquely named village because she had lived here during her nurse training before her marriage.

Life was completely different in 36 BB. No one judged her for her divorce or pitied her for being a single parent. All she got from her hospital staff and neighbours was love and support. On some days when she would be busy catering to the patients, her friends would take care of the babies. 'Everyone knows Jasbeer in our village, not for her past but her affection and friendly nature towards everyone. She is always ready to help and at times she even goes beyond her duty hours to serve the patients,' said Vakil Singh, Sarpanch of the village.

Jasbeer's day would typically start early in the morning around five. After doing the household chores, she would pack lunch for all four of them and leave for work. From early on, she had taught the sisters to be there for each other and always stick together. If one refused to go to school, the other two followed the suit.

After working in an eight-hour shift, Jasbeer would return in the evening and help the trio with their school work.

Although it was a fixed routine, Jasbeer broke down often.

'I was doing everything that usually men do, whether it was repairing an electronic item, changing light bulbs, or doing the heavy lifting chores. Even in terms of finances, I struggled in the initial days. I had to compromise on my daughters' needs. I had to decide what was important—school fees or food. These tough decisions helped me get stronger,' said Jasbeer.

However, she did a decent job at hiding her troubles, said Pradeep, 'We complained how other parents came to pick their children. She never dismissed us and would assure us that the next day she would try.'

Being a single parent, she ensured there was an open communication channel with the triplets. She informed them about her divorce, including the abortion episode when they got older. Jasbeer always takes them in confidence and teaches them things in an age-appropriate manner.

Jasbeer's life has been nothing short of a movie. So what kept her going despite all the adversities?

'*Main ek kisan ki beti hoon* (I am a farmer's daughter) so being internally strong comes naturally. We toil hard under the sun to provide food to people. If a farmer's family can fight storms and droughts, we can do it. We believe in ourselves and stay firm always,' she concludes.

Today, Jasbeer is content with her life and lives happily in 36 BB along with Mandeep. Sandeep and Pradeep have moved to Amritsar and Chandigarh, respectively, for their jobs.

Although on the cusp of retirement, Jasbeer hopes to serve as a nurse for as long as she can, even if it means working independently.

Coming Out, Into Acceptance

Vidya Raja

'Making the decision to have a child is momentous. It is to decide forever to have your heart go walking around outside your body,' wrote Elizabeth Stone.

As a parent to two boys, there are several instances in which I feel like this quote comes rushing to me. During a freewheeling conversation with celebrated LGBTQIA+ activist, Sushant Divgikar (they/them), I could not set aside my 'parent' hat.

They speak of coming out, the support of their family and their drag queen persona Rani-Ko-HE-Nur.

'I am blessed and highly favoured to be born into a family like mine,' began Sushant. They tell me that they have only good memories with their parents. Sushant's father was unlike any other, who would never see a reason why they could not get themselves a Barbie doll. 'I found them to be so beautifully dressed and I was automatically drawn to the grace. Never once did I hear my father question my choice,' they added.

While friends would make fun of why a 'boy' would want to play with a Barbie doll, their family was rather supportive and that gave Sushant strength. 'I was never judged at home. I was always allowed to express myself differently from other boys. They believed that kids should never be subjected to any kind of conditioning whatsoever,' said the thirty-year-old.

This was in the early 1990s when conversations and dialogues were not as open as they are today. 'Today, my story is out there. However, when I was growing up, I had no access to such interviews or people even. My sense of strength came from my parents, who never had any rules based on gender,' Sushant said.

Coming Out: Not an Earth-Shattering Revelation

Pradeep Divgikar, Sushant's father, was rather clear in his thought process. He viewed both his children with the same lens. There was never a question about how one of his children was straight and the other gay. A lot of the confidence that Sushant exudes comes from their parents, who have stood by them like a rock.

Speaking about their father, Sushant said, 'Coming from a conservative family and to say that I will be the best father I can and let my children be, was perhaps the best gift he could have given us. I continue to live with my parents and while that comes as a shock to many, it's a choice I have made—to live with them until they are around and I love it.'

In their signature animated style, Sushant added, 'I remember a conversation with my mother where she told me that she wished I would become an architect and here I was telling her that I wanted to pursue psychology. My father stepped in and said I should study whatever I felt like and not bother about anything else.'

Sushant has a very interesting story of coming out to their family. The first person in the family that Sushant came out to was their older brother, Karan, who according to Sushant, couldn't keep anything in his stomach. 'He promptly went to my father and told him that I was gay. My father, in his indomitable style, asked my brother what it was to him if I were gay. All this was happening when I was just about eighteen,' they said. Subsequent conversations with their father were all about reiterating that they wasn't 'straight' or 'gay', they was just his child.

'I knew they loved me and would do anything for me but I must admit even I was in awe of this reaction,' they said. Coming out to their mother was a rather subdued event. 'I remember it was one afternoon when she was immersed in watching her daily serial, when I interrupted and told her I had something important to share. She actually shushed me and asked me to wait until the commercial break to speak.'

Sushant sat there quietly waiting for the commercial break. 'Here I was, wanting to tell her something so monumental about myself and she was worried about what the actor on screen would do. Imagine,' they laughed. Sushant pestered her some more until she muted the television and asked them what all the fuss was about. 'She looked at me and said if this was about me being gay, she knew already. I had expected drama, even thought she might faint when I came out to her. She surprised me and how. What a rock star she has been.'

They also recount how after this brief conversation she went back to watching her serial, like nothing had happened.

'That day over lunch, my mother told me the one thing I always remember—Never make anyone feel lesser than me for any reason or harm anyone else for any reason. In the same breath, she also made it a point to add that just like my brother wasn't allowed to bring girls into his room, I wouldn't be allowed to bring any boys home,' Sushant said, again with peals of laughter.

If there was ever a movie to be made on Sushant's life, they add, it would be a riot of emotions and laughter all the way. 'It really is all about accepting people and your children just as they are.'

The Making of Rani-Ko-HE-Nur

'To be honest, I would say that I have been a drag performer since my school days. I would sing in two voices and was always good on stage, so was the natural choice for competitions representing the school,' they said. Since Sushant studied in an all-boys school, at every competition or performance, the female role would automatically be given to Sushant. 'People were always impressed with me. I subsequently even trained in dancing,' added the activist.

They also learnt music by watching stalwarts like Whitney Houston, Anita Franklin, Michael Jackson, Freddy Mercury, and Mariah Carey. And closer home, they were inspired by Usha Uthup, Falguni Pathak, Asha Bhonsle, Alka Yagnik, and so many more. 'This meant that my repertoire and genre in singing was just so wide. I have amalgamated all these voices and worked on creating something very unique. I learnt vicariously,' said Sushant.

In 2015, Sushant performed officially as a drag artist for the first time. This was for *Merchant of Venice*, a stage production directed by Vikram Kapadia. 'The response to that was phenomenal and thereafter, I hosted the Kashish Queer

Film Festival in Mumbai and performed before the legendary Sir Ian McKellen. Through my initial performances, however, I had not taken on the name of Rani-Ko-HE-Nur yet,' they said. This led to Sushant getting various offers to perform and it started from there.

In 2017, Sushant found themselves in Delhi, where they were invited to perform at a private event. 'It was after this party when Keshav Suri, the Executive Director of Lalit Hospitality, christened me as "Rani". To this I added, Ko-HE-Nur (Kohinoor) and this became Rani-Ko-HE-Nur. The rest as they say is history,' said the drag artist. It has been fifteen glorious years of Sushant being in the entertainment industry and they continue to enthral people, whether in their drag persona or otherwise.

Under all the glitz and glamour, Sushant holds a masters degree in psychology and has been a topper not just in academics but also in sports.

A true inspiration for the many who are silently suffering and contemplating the unfair social consequences of coming out, Sushant said, 'If you have the joy of raising a child, cherish that. Having a different gender or orientation is absolutely no reason for you to abandon your child. Your job as parents is to accept and love your child unconditionally. What they do in their life's journey is up to them. Do not live your dreams through them.'

Section II

When The Going Gets Tough

*'I can be changed by what happens to me.
But I refuse to be reduced to it.'*

Maya Angelou

A Voice for the Voiceless

Gopi Karelia

A pregnant Mamta Devi, who was in labour, clenched her bedside handles tightly to overcome every contraction. Lying in a government hospital in Jharkhand's Koderma district, the pain was so unbearable that she felt like separating herself from her womb. As she tried to focus on the beautiful miracle of birth, she was asked to wait some more. After what seemed like a lifetime, Devi was forced to shift to a private hospital as the government doctor in question had neglected Devi and had left for the day to attend her private practice.

While Devi had a normal delivery, giving birth to a healthy baby, the operation fees of the private facility pushed her family into a debt of Rs 50,000. This episode of medical negligence occurred in 2015, but no less than a year later she was compensated Rs 1,00,000.

Devi was pleasantly surprised to know that a man called Onkar Vishwakarma had read about her plight in a newspaper clipping and filed a case with the National Human Rights Commission (NHRC) on her behalf. Today, Onkar is the voice for several strangers like Devi who have been wronged by the system.

'The beauty of NHRC is that an individual can file a case on behalf of anyone without actually knowing them. In *suo moto* cases, a newspaper clipping, victim's statement, police complaint can be counted as evidence,' said Jharkhand-based Onkar, an activist who runs an NGO called Sangram.

This philanthropist fights for the voiceless based on newspaper clippings and Devi's case was his first major human rights case.

'When I met Devi she was surprised and relieved,' said Onkar, adding, 'The process of filing online and offline is simple. Once I get the judgment, I track down the person and give them the judgment copy which they can use to get the compensation.'

In the last ten years, the thirty-two-year-old has filed several cases with the NHRC and won around fifteen of those cases. Seven people he has fought for, including Devi, have received a cumulative compensation worth Rs 13,00,000. These cases include police brutality, medical negligence, job security, malnutrition-related deaths, and more.

However, the right to express freedom and self-dignity were alien concepts for a young Onkar who hailed from a tiny village called Domachach. Having been physically abused and forced to work for the better part of his childhood, Onkar became a helping hand that he was never privy to.

Absence of Dignity

Onkar was six when he witnessed his inebriated father physically assaulting his cancer-stricken mother for the first time. Soon, domestic violence became an acceptable norm, almost like a ritual in the house. So, when he worked as a child labourer in a garage, he didn't oppose his employer's beating.

When his father finally abandoned their family, taking most of their belongings, including their food, he internalized the guilt. His mother took up menial jobs like ferrying passengers on the bullock cart, while his grandmother cut grass. Life was hard all around. The family spent the next couple of years in despair and extreme poverty. Together, they made just enough money to afford food. Their monthly income was between Rs 75 and Rs 100 in the 1990s. 'I was not granted any respect and fair pay even in my second job as a mechanic. I thought I didn't deserve it until education came to my rescue,' he said.

It was only after clearing Class 8 did Onkar start dreaming big. 'Blame it on the feudalism or caste system, dehumanizing menial jobs like domestic work, garbage collection and manual scaling is a deep-rooted practice in India. What is even more appalling is that even today, most of us turn a blind eye to the dignity of labour,' he said.

Unfortunately, his taxing work schedule hampered his education, and he couldn't pass his boards in 2003. 'I was back to square one—working in a stone crusher plant for the next couple of years and reappearing for boards with my friends' encouragement. This time, my intent was different, and I wanted to prove my worth. I studied hard and passed. That was the turning point in my life,' said Onkar.

He then decided to work in the social welfare sector to uplift the downtrodden and the exploited by pursuing a degree in Sociology Honours from Vinoba Bhave University, Hazaribagh, Jharkhand.

Unfolding the Bitter Truth

In 2009, he started taking tuitions for school children to pay for his graduation. As part of college projects, he joined an NGO that advocated for the rights of children and farmers.

'My eyes were opened to society's bitter truth. It is so unfair that the perpetrators and the exploited continue normalizing discriminatory and unlawful practices. Here, I learnt my biggest lesson that every person has a right to express and a right to dissent. After learning how to use constitutional rights, government welfare schemes and more, I started my NGO in 2008,' said Onkar.

His first initiative was for the upliftment of the endangered Birhor tribal community that resides in a fragmented forest near North Chotanagpur. He helped the forest-dependent families access Aadhar cards, enrol children in schools, avail farming-related government schemes for alternative livelihoods, and other basic facilities such as water and electricity. After working with the deprived community for more than two years, Onkar found his true calling: 'Several Birhor families had lost their loved ones due to lack of healthcare facilities. There was no compensation or monetary relief given. In 2011, I collaborated with a Varanasi-based People's Vigilance Committee on Human Rights (PVCHR) to file cases.' From 2013, he began filing rights violation cases independently.

'Coming from a marginalized background, Onkar understood what we were doing,' said Onkar's mentor, Dr Lenin Raghuvanshi, CEO of PVCHR. 'He is very hardworking, sincere, passionate, and committed to working on diverse issues. He is a quick learner who refused to bow down in the face of adversities. I am very proud of his work,' he added.

Being the Change in the Face of Threats

Today, Onkar trudges on dangerous paths with constant threats. While in the beginning, it was hard on his wife and children, now he has learnt how to tackle the threats with legal measures.

'There are times when I feel like leaving this profession and settling for something that is more stable and safe. But looking back at my own journey, I feel it's all worth it and it feels right to continue helping. I am currently pursuing law so that I can go one step further in shielding human rights,' he said with a smile.

For each case, Onkar follows a very meticulous filing and tracking process. Before approaching the NHRC, he follows the progress of the case through news reports. In one of his ongoing cases, he is following up with the help of local journalists to get compensation to the family of a man who was killed in a 'fake' encounter in 2019.

One of the most significant cases of Onkar's career came in 2017 which made national headlines. Baidyanath Ravidas, forty-three, a resident of Dhanbad district died of starvation after not consuming food for seven days. A rickshaw-puller by profession, he had made several trips to get a ration card for subsidized food but to no avail.

Based on the fact-finding report by Jharkhand-based lawyers Shadab Ansari and Mumtaz Ansari, Onkar filed a case with the NHRC. In early 2020, the commission directed the then-Jharkhand Government to pay Rs 1,00,000 compensation to Baidyanath's kin. It was the first time the State Government gave compensation for death due to hunger.

'Once the commission directs the concerned entity or state government, the onus of ensuring it reaches the victim falls on them. In some cases, either it is delayed or not given. In such cases, we follow up with the district administration and get the media's attention till the family gets the money,' he said.

Being extraordinarily dedicated to his work and compassionate towards others are attributes that make him human to the utmost degree.

'We are far better individuals than we give ourselves credit for,' he adds.

Reaching for the Stars

Sanchari Pal

Stories of people overcoming adversity resonate with something deep within us. The parts of us that hope our future is not determined by destiny but by our hard work. One such incredible story of resilience and inspiration belongs to IAS officer Vijay Kulange.

Born in the tiny village of Ralegan in Maharashtra's Ahmadnagar district to a father who worked as a tailor and a mother who worked as a daily-wage worker on farms, Vijay grew up seeing his parents toil all day long to make both ends meet.

Earning just about Rs 200 a day, his parents were constantly worried about providing their children with two square meals a day. Money was always scarce, and even bare necessities were unimaginable. The only thing Vijay had ever had in abundance during childhood was a burning desire to lessen his parents' worries and to do them proud. And all through his life, he did just that.

'Despite living in such hardship, both my parents were firm in their shared belief that this situation would not determine how far their children would go in life. From a young age, my parents taught me the importance of education and how it could change our lives for the better. My sister and I may have never had any toys in our childhood, but we never lacked the stationery required to attend the local Zilla Parishad school. The school was always a priority,' said Vijay.

A voracious reader, Vijay was always among the top performers at school—in the Class 10 and 12 board examinations. Having grown up in a drought-prone village with high poverty levels and very little development, he decided to become a doctor and serve the underprivileged. However, despite getting a college seat to pursue MBBS, he had to drop this dream due to the family's financial circumstances. 'We were still living in poverty, and I needed to start earning as soon as possible. The seven–eight years needed to make a career in the medical profession was something I couldn't afford. I had a younger sister, and as was common in those days, my parents were worried about her marriage. Plus, we would have needed to take a huge loan. Any failure would have meant disaster for the family', said Vijay.

Vijay decided to do something that would lead to a job immediately.

Choosing a Diploma in Education (DEd) after careful consideration, he completed it and joined as a primary teacher at a government school in the nearby Nevasa Taluka within six months. A steady salary from this job went a long way in assuaging his parents' worries while also helping him do his graduation via distance education.

But Vijay always felt he could have achieved more. His father also sensed this constant thought in Vijay's mind and encouraged him to prepare for the state civil service exam. 'My father would tell me that studying for an exam is never a loss. It is always a win–win. If I qualify and get a better job, it would be great. But even if I didn't, I would have gained precious knowledge while still having my current job. He also pointed out that it would help me become a better teacher as well,' recalls Vijay.

These words would go on to help Vijay several times in his journey. Inspired by them, he decided to prepare for Maharashtra State Civil Service (MPSC) exam. Covering the vast syllabus wasn't an easy task, but he persevered, sticking to a strict routine of working by day and studying by night.

In his first two attempts, Vijay failed to crack the exam. Naturally, he was disappointed, but his parents never let his spirits drop. On the contrary, they constantly bolstered up his belief in himself, so Vijay decided to quit his job and dedicate all his time to a final attempt. The decision paid off when he cracked the MPSC exam on his third attempt and became a Sales Tax Inspector in Ahmadnagar. In the following year, he also cleared the exam for the post of Tehsildar. 'With every success in these exams, my confidence kept increasing. Also, during this time, I met the then-District Collector of Ahmadnagar, IAS officer Sanjeev Kumar, who encouraged me to attempt the UPSC Civil Service Examination. I took up his suggestion—despite getting very little study leave for preparations,' said Vijay.

Vijay decided not to take any coaching and would study hard in the little time he would get before and after his duty hours. Since he still struggled with English, he chose to give the exam in Marathi, which made preparation more challenging since little study material was available in the language. But, as they say, fortune favours the brave. In 2012, he cracked UPSC CSE in his first attempt and earned the rank of an IAS officer.

When asked what was crucial in his success, Vijay said, 'It was the confidence lent by my father's words and the safety net of my job that let me attempt UPSC CSE with very little fear or pressure. I wasn't worried about not qualifying. I just wanted to give my best. What also held me in good stead was five years of making notes for the state civil service exam.'

Vijay's first posting as an IAS officer was in Odisha's Dhenkanal district. He has since penned a Marathi book 'Aajcha Diwas Maza', where he describes his struggles, journey, and the sacrifices his parents had made to raise their children. Today, he lives with his proud parents and continues to work proactively towards transforming Odisha. During the pandemic, Vijay earned much public acclaim for kickstarting a slew of popular initiatives as the collector of Ganjam. This district has been hit by Cyclones Fani, Yaas, and Amphan.

'A large number of migrant workers from this district work in Surat and Mumbai. During the first wave of the pandemic in India, four lakh of them returned home at once, making it a massive task to trace, quarantine, test, and treat the positive cases. We began providing food packets, sanitizers and transportation to Temporary Medical Camps (TMC) for a mandatory quarantine stay to each of these returnees. An incentive of Rs 15,000 (to be given post-quarantine) was also announced. And since most of these TMCs had been set up in schools, we used the skills of the migrant labourers to beautify and repair all the school campuses—as employment under MGNREGS,' shares Vijay,

Ganjam was among India's first districts to promulgate Section 144 of CrPc to restrict gatherings of five or more people. In addition, all Tahsildars of the district were declared as 'Incident Commanders' under the Epidemic Diseases Act to enforce the prevention guidelines. A fine enforced wearing a mask, and special squads ensured that shopkeepers followed social-distancing norms in their stores.

Even though these measures helped the district stay Covid-free for almost two months, Vijay boosted the district's health infrastructure to handle an increased load. A 200-bed COVID hospital with fifty ICU beds was prepared in fifteen days by Vijay and his team, who worked round-the-clock to make this happen. Three other COVID hospitals, eight COVID Care Centres, and a 20 KL Liquid Medical Oxygen plant were set up. Door-to-door screening was also conducted in the district that has a population of over thirty-five lakh, with Rs 50 lakh offered to the family of every frontline worker who lost their lives while doing their duty.

Even when the cyclonic storm Yaas hit Ganjam in May 2021, Vijay managed to keep the district running with timely evacuations and equipping the cyclone shelters with an adequate supply of medical oxygen, hospital beds and doctors for Covid-19 patients.

All this was done when most of the country was struggling to meet the logistical challenges that a deadly second wave posed.

Vijay also launched an initiative under which anybody who provided a tip-off about an upcoming child marriage would get a cash reward of Rs 5000. The informer's identity would be kept a secret. Unsurprisingly, the idea was a resounding success—38 child marriages were prevented in a few months!

'Though many people know about such child marriages being organized, they rarely inform the administration, fearing backlash from the families and the village leaders. The anonymity and cash award we offered motivated these people to come forward and flag cases, thus saving many young girls,' said Vijay.

Vijay followed this by revamping 60 government schools—sanitation and hygiene were improved, staff requirements were filled, smart labs and libraries were installed, and their functioning was monitored. He also launched the 'Jala Ghanti' (Water Bell) initiative to help students stay hydrated and make drinking water frequently a habit.

Having had personally witnessed the difficulties of farmers and farm workers back in his village, Vijay has also launched the TARA scheme to increase farm incomes through crop diversification and training in techniques such as mulching, moisture conservation, micro-irrigation, and more.

In fact, during the pandemic, the Ganjam district used MGNREGS funds worth over Rs 50 crore to help marginalized farmers improve their earnings.

The best example of this stunning impact is the story of B. Chakradhara Reddy, a poor farmer who makes a living by selling milk from his four cows. Due to a scarcity of fodder and the lack of a shed to shelter his cows, milk production fell drastically during the pandemic, leaving him struggling to make ends meet till he applied for the TARA scheme.

'Without spending any of my savings or taking any loans, I got a cattle shed, a compost pit, a soak pit, a fodder production unit, and a farm pond—all through MGNREGS funds released through the TARA scheme. As a result, my cows are much healthier and producing double the milk they would give earlier. I am also using their dung to grow vegetables and fodder. As for the pond, I have learnt the basics of pisciculture, and I will start practising it soon,' said B. Chakradhara, relief and gratitude evident in his voice.

The list of IAS Vijay Kulange's initiatives is a very, very long one—he is also the brain behind 'Rajaswa Rath', an innovative idea that takes revenue services such as updation of land records and issuing of certificates to the doorsteps of people. All district collectors in Odisha have now been told to emulate Ganjam's example and implement this idea.

While this infectious passion for public service has fetched him widespread respect in the official circles, his instinctive thoughtfulness has endeared him deeply to the people of Odisha. Even apart from his work, his journey of chasing his dream with a single-minded focus is nothing short of inspirational.

However, he wears this praise lightly. 'It wasn't easy, but I was willing to work hard for it and was determined to succeed. That is what got me through,' concludes the IAS officer.

For Love for Their Children

Jovita Aranha

Try hailing an autorickshaw from Mumbai's Bhandup station to Sonapur. The usually indifferent driver is likely to recoil in horror and judgement. It's best to walk the thirty minutes from the station to North Mumbai's lesser known red-light district, where underworld crime syndicates run prostitution rings. This is where spine-chilling and heart-wrenching stories come alive.

'*Ab toh buddhi ho gayi hun, toh mushkil hai kamaai,*' said Farida. She is older now, so it's harder to make money.

While Roopmati entered the sex trade only two years ago, Farida has been in the business for almost two decades. None of their family members knows that they work as commercial sex workers. Except for Farida's second husband, a rickshaw driver in the city, with whom she has a nine-year-old daughter.

The veteran of the two continues speaking about how the sex trade no longer runs the way it did ten years ago. The market that once fetched them almost a lakh a month has now seen their earnings dwindle to less than Rs 10,000–15,000.

As you enter Sonapur, you walk through a narrow lane, feeling as if the walls on either side will close in on you at any time. A gutter runs from the centre of the gully, parting the rows of homes on either side, which are painted in bright shades of blue. Women sit in the verandahs, looking at those passing by.

One washes her face, three detangle their hair, laughing away to jokes privy only to them as older women look on. Dressed in low-neck nighties, decked in gold, with well-plucked eyebrows, a hint of blush on their cheeks and bright red lipstick adorning their lips, they wait for the first customers of the day.

'The rules are clear. The sex worker cannot leave the brothel or refuse a customer.'

Farida gives a sneak peek of her place of work.

Each room in a brothel, depending on its size, has space for three to eight sex workers. In contrast to other cramped rooms in the vicinity, the dormitory-like hall has wooden bunks rising to the ceiling.

All the women who live in that particular dorm work there as well. Many of them are unwed mothers. Their children, who are too young to understand what is happening, sleep in the corner or under the bunks. Only a thin veil of a curtain separates them from their mothers who trade their bodies to give them a better life.

Like Farida, the stories of many others who work in red-light areas across Mumbai, including the oldest district at Kamathipura, are similar.

Rescue Foundation is an anti-trafficking NGO. Operating for the last 30 years, the NGO rescues trafficked women and girls and rehabilitates them. It has impacted more than 5000 girls and women to date.

Girls as young as nine are sold for Rs 50,000 to Rs 3,00,000, while older women are sold for much less. They come from across the country and even beyond the borders, from Nepal and Bangladesh. Their abject poverty makes them and their families vulnerable to fake promises and hollow opportunities for big money in cities.

And for some, it is their chance of finding love.

Triveni Acharya is the co-founder of Rescue Foundation. She said that when newly-trafficked girls are brought in, they are put in what is called a *pinjra* or a cage. Triveni adds how the pinjra still exists in Kamathipura. It is a wooden cell or bunk where the victim is kept until she is brainwashed into becoming a seasoned sex worker.

While underground elements benefit from a brothel, *gharwalis* or housekeepers run the place. Often, she's an older woman who has been in the trade all her life.

'Ninety-nine per cent of brothel keepers are women who were trafficked at some stage in their lives. Unable to escape, they were brutalized and brainwashed into thinking that they were outcasts. And that their bodies were mere commodities. Because many of them were rejected by their families and societies at large, they became veteran sex workers. And as they grow older, they take up the reigns of the brothel,' said Triveni.

The housekeepers are feared and keep the workers on a tight leash. They cook, wash, and keep the rooms clean, ensuring that the girls do not escape.

'The gharwalis use different methods to make the newbies give in to the trade. From coaxing them with sweet, comforting words to pressuring them meanly. Statements like "We have paid so much money to buy you. How can you just leave?"

are common. If the girls don't listen, they are intimidated, gang-raped, and emotionally traumatized. Women who are trafficked with their daughters are sexually abused in front of each other. They are starved, burned around their breast and genital areas with cigarette butts, chained with fetters, and forced to undergo sterilization, so they don't procreate. Many of them don't even see sunlight for days.'

Despite the torture, some refuse to give up. They are told that if they work hard enough and recover the amount they were sold for, they will be free to go.

The ones who escape are transferred to other brothels where they are tortured further. They are put under *bandhan*. During this time, they work to recover the money which was spent to 'buy' them. They don't earn a penny, just food, clothing, and accommodation. 'The rules are clear. The sex worker cannot leave the brothel or refuse a customer. Once the principal sum of her *karja* or loan is recovered, she gets paid half the money. Healthcare is an additional expense.'

Though most women leave the brothel once they have paid off their loans, many can't find employment elsewhere due to illiteracy. Being rejected by their own families makes things worse.

They return, this time for themselves, to make money.

If Have to Sell My Blood, I Will Do It to Educate My Kids

Back in Sonapur, a woman in her late thirties, Roopmati is dressed in a bright nightgown and an equally colourful dupatta. Not a hair peeks out of her tight bun. Her eyebrows are thick and well-brushed, the effort to maintain them is visible. Her lips are lined with a subtle shade of lipstick in stark contrast to the other women. A large bindi adorns her forehead. Her ears have multiple piercings, each adorned with a gold earring. She also wears a mangalsutra underneath the dupatta.

She grew up in Khedegaon, in rural Maharashtra. Fourth of seven siblings born to a homemaker and a marginal farmer, she never lived in a pucca home, just a shed with makeshift tin sheet walls.

When she was merely seven, her father passed away. It was the beginning of the worst period of her life.

She said, 'My mother was illiterate and couldn't afford to send me to school. I envied the girls who went to school every day, while I toiled in the harsh sun from 10 a.m. to 5 p.m. for a meagre wage of Rs 10. And yet, a square meal was a luxury. Sometimes when the flour was not enough for all eight of us, my *aai* (mother) would add water and make transparent rotis. We'd joke that if we looked closely, we could see the silhouette of the person sitting on the opposite side. I thought marriage would relieve me of my poverty. But I was wrong.'

Her voice is husky and guarded. She was married at an early age to an older man, who worked as a driver. 'He was illiterate, with elderly parents to care for and no proper home. His monthly salary was Rs 10,000 for the longest time. So I did household chores for five years to earn a menial sum. While this was enough to run the household and pay medical bills for his parents, it fell short of funding the education for my kids. I couldn't bear to watch them live the same life as me.'

A neighbour told her about a work opportunity in Mumbai, and Roopmati set out for the city of dreams. But the neighbour had lied to her.

'I am sure he earned a commission for bringing me here. If I were educated, I could at least move a pen or do some work for a company to fund my children's education. But what could an illiterate woman do? My husband and children would hate me if they ever find out that I am doing sex work. But I have no other option. I will not let the lives of my children be ruined like mine. I won't let my daughter be pushed to the extremes for being uneducated like I was.'

Her earnings have now helped her purchase a home in Pune.

Roopmati's eyes well up when she talks about how she's spent over Rs 3 lakh earned from the trade on the education of her two kids—a son and a daughter. While her daughter is now studying at a private-cum-NGO-run agricultural college in Pune, her son has returned from the residential school he was studying at to stay with her husband and in-laws.

She sounds troubled as she speaks about them. She reveals that the partner NGO she entrusted the education of her children had conned her. Despite spending lakhs of rupees over the last three years, Roopmati was never given a receipt. The children were admitted as orphans to save the costs of education, food, and accommodation. The truth never came out because every time she spoke to her children, the warden at the hostel would put the phone on speaker. The administration there even put up a fight to send the children home during their Christmas vacation last year despite it being the first time they were returning home.

'They knew that I was working as a commercial sex worker to educate my children. When they refused to send the children, and referred to me as their relative and not as their mother, I was shocked. I had to pay an additional Rs 9000 to bring them home,' she shares.

And that's not all.

When Roopmati's daughter finally came home that Christmas, she burst out crying, sharing the mean things the hostel staff kept telling her. They even made the children clean toilets, work in the fields, and fetch groceries from the market. Often, her son was bullied and beaten up, and even made to beg.

'Once when they refused to eat dinner, one of the staff told them, "*Madam, yeh dhandewali ke bacchon ke bahut natak hai.* (Madam, the kids of this prostitute are too fussy)." I was aghast. My heart broke as my daughter kept asking me what a dhandewali meant. I told her it refers to vendors who sell goods. I don't think she was convinced.'

Roopmati wants to one day leave the red-light area. She said, 'I am adamant to clear my pending loan of Rs 30,000 and get out of here as soon as possible. I feel my husband and daughter suspect that I work here. But I just want my kids to get educated and never see the life that I have lived. '*Agar badan ka khoon bhi bechna pade, toh karunga. Lekin mere baccha log ko padhayega. Yeh line mein nahi aane dega.* (Even if I have to sell my own blood to educate my children, I will. I won't let my daughter step into my line of work).'

My Daughter is Nine. She Dreams of Becoming a Doctor or an IPS Officer

As Roopmati shares her story, Farida quietly wipes away her tears. Her reaction comes from a place of deep hurt, not just for her friend, Roopmati, but also her own life. Her lost dreams, her yearning for her daughter.

In her early forties, Farida is one of the veteran sex workers in the area. Her face is devoid of any make up. Just a tiny bindi wit her hair in a messy bun.

Her Hindi has a heavy Bengali accent.

Kolkata was anything but the city of joy for her. Her family was very poor. She was married and had three sons, but was soon abandoned by her husband.

In time, she grew estranged from her in-laws who took her sons away from her. She then came to Mumbai twenty years ago, and has spent most of those years in the sex trade.

'In the first few years, I did household chores at Sanpada. But the money was barely enough. I found love for the second time thirteen years ago, and remarried.'

Farida's husband is an autorickshaw driver and they have a nine-year-old daughter, who has been studying in a residential school in Pune. She tells me that her husband knows about her line of work.

She wishes there was another way of funding her daughter's education. But it's not easy. '*Bolna asaan hai. Jab zarurat tha tab kisine madat nahi ki. Toh mai haath kyun failau? Main apne paise ka kamata hun, khata hun, aur baccha ko padata hun.* (It is easy to tell someone not to do sex work. But when I was in dire need of money, nobody helped me. Now, why should I beg? I earn my money, fill my stomach, and fund my daughter's education.)'

After spending two decades in the business, as she approaches her forties, she doesn't have big dreams. And they aren't even for her, but her daughter.

'My husband stays in Uttar Pradesh. When the time is right, I will move there with my daughter. We'll start a new life. For now, I just want her to complete her education.'

She adds, 'Choosing this life wasn't easy. I may appear composed, but I can't sleep at night. Sometimes, I lay in bed awake until 4 a.m., thinking about what my life has become. But I wonder if it would have been different if I was born in a middle-class family, got an education, found love, and raised my child differently. But when I look at the glint and delight in my daughter's eyes every time I visit her, nothing else matters. What matters is that she is getting educated. She will never live the life that I did.'

Farida visits her daughter twice every month. She boards a bus late on Fridays so that they can spend the whole of Saturday together. Naturally, she looks forward to the visits.

'I stay up on Fridays cooking everything she likes. You should see the happiness on her face, as she devours everything. She is studying in Class 2 in an English-medium school and tells me that her dream is to become a doctor or an IPS officer. Every time I pay her fee, she signs for me. For the longest time, her teachers thought I couldn't speak. So she told them, "My mummy finds it difficult to interact in English and Marathi. So please speak to her in Hindi." The teachers are all very fond of her. They say she is a bright girl and that she will achieve something big in life. And at times like these, I can't stop the tears.'

'Won't Lose My Life to Earn an Extra Buck, Right?'

Both women are aware that they have to be careful about protecting themselves against HIV and other STDs.

Roopmati said, 'We place our safety before anything else. We have watched young women and girls suffer and die from unprotected sex. So our rules for our customers are clear. If someone asks for unsafe sex, we tell them to leave. We don't engage in unprotected sex with any customer no matter where they come from or who they are.'

Who are their customers?

Farida answers that they come from all backgrounds. From a rickshaw driver to a cop. Some have families, others stay alone in the city to scrape a living.

'They reach our doorstep for their needs,' she said. 'For us, it isn't about intimacy. Just a transaction. Some pay Rs 500, others Rs 1000. Once a man tried to push me into having unprotected sex. He offered to pay Rs 5000. I told him to either put on a condom and give me my regular rate, or leave, and that I wouldn't consent even if he paid me a lakh. *Do rupayee ke liye apni jaan thodi gavayega!* (Won't lose my life to earn an extra buck, right?). Only if we live will we be able to work for a few more years and help our children.'

'The Bazaar No Longer Runs Like It Did'

The red-light areas in Mumbai no longer make the business they once did.

Law enforcement now strikes down on brothels. But while the brothels continue in privacy, they have to protect themselves too.

And the attitudes of sex workers doesn't aid their dwindling incomes.

Roopmati said, 'Many of them transfer here from other brothels. Since this place is not as exploitative, their attitude changes. In the greed to gain more money, many of them loot customers and hit them. The gharwalis here also assist them. They abuse the customers and blackmail them. This inconveniences the rest of us who are working hard. But what can we do?'

Not much, and life goes on for many of them.

Triveni of Rescue Foundation acknowledges that the law on commercial sex work isn't always clear.

'It is a grey area,' she said.

'There are several loopholes. While there are clear laws on the trafficking of humans for sex trade, there is no clarity on the exploitation of women above eighteen who are living and earning in prostitution. Besides, the social stigma from thirty years ago still exists. So, many of these women have nowhere to go. But with the new anti-trafficking law that is under consideration, rules on rescue, rehabilitation, and compensation of trafficked individuals as well as exploited commercial sex workers will become clearer.'

Fear, Risk, Betrayal: The Carousel Keeps Turning

Rescue Foundation also handles in-brothel counselling. Leveraging their pool of informers, investigators, and spies, they conduct raids and rescue operations in red-light areas. The investigators put their lives on the line and disguise themselves as customers. They focus on minors, and once they are left alone in the room with the girl, they counsel her.

Sometimes, it takes multiple visits to the brothels to build trust with the minors, who are scared for their lives and have already lived the worst form of betrayal. The interaction is risky—not only for the minor but also the investigator whose identity is protected at all costs.

Triveni said, 'Once the trust is built, the girls open up about their sorrows and insecurities. It is only when she gives us her consent and agrees to cooperate with us that our informers report back to us. After a few days, we file an FIR and raid the brothel with the police. We do not enter the red-light district without police protection.'

But the job is not without risks. One of their investigators was stabbed five years ago. Triveni lost her husband, the leading founder of Rescue Foundation, fifteen years ago. She suspects that his accident was framed, but that hasn't stopped her from continuing her work.

Do women always cooperate or have there been instances where they backed out?

She answers, 'Sometimes, girls change their statements, lie about their age, or state that they are working out of choice. Even though they do this out of fear, there isn't much we can do for them after this. Many are stuck in the cycle of prostitution because they are convinced there is no life for them in the outside world. But at other times, when we go to rescue one girl, several others step up.'

Once rescued, the girls move into the Foundation's residential facility and go through a series of processes to regain stability and balance. Apart from legal proceedings to punish their perpetrators, the survivors also attend counselling sessions and therapy to deal with the trauma. They are enrolled in training courses, and provided with education and employment.

Like Rescue Foundation, Purnata, an NGO that works to rehabilitate former sex workers, too, works with law enforcement agencies on prevention and rescue. As their website says, their mission is 'Protecting the vulnerable. Restoring the stolen'. Their team does surveillance of major railway stations in the city and rescues children in transit at railway stations and other nodal points.

Purnata has rescued over thirty victims of trafficking, including fifteen minors. It has rehabilitated and reintegrated twelve survivors into mainstream society. It supports them by helping them find love and get married. It has also ensured safe housing for twenty-five children who were at risk of being trafficked. Its awareness programmes have reached more than 50,000 people.

Purnata has a centre for women in Sonapur where they hold training, counselling sessions, and events. They also run a day-care centre for kids, providing quality education, nutritious meals, and activities to promote hygiene and good health.

For Farida and Roopmati, however, life will continue as usual. But talking with each other helps, even though they don't share their sorrows often. 'Sometimes, we wish to share our stories with people who care. But nobody has time. In fact, they laugh and mock us. It's easier to judge dhandewalis, isn't it?' said Roopmati.

But She Bloomed

Gopi Karelia

'I was buried alive for nearly seven hours before my mother and aunt dug my grave and pulled me out after hearing my incessant cries. I do not know if it was the grass covering the soil that helped me breathe or simply a fighting spirit that gave a less-than-one-day-old baby from Ajmer's Kotda village the strength. But I refused to give up on myself,' said Gulabo Sapera, who bloomed in the patriarchal landscape of Rajasthan and went on to create history in more ways than one.

Years later, this girl with an indomitable spirit was featured in a magazine. But her name was misspelt and, since then, to the world, she came to be known as Gulabo—the sensational Sapera (or Kalbelia) dancer from Pushkar who could bend in unimaginable ways.

When she turned one, Gulabo, originally named Dhanvati, fell seriously ill and the doctors almost gave up on her, but once again she fought hard to live. A rose was placed next to her in the clinic, and seeing the flower as a sign of goodwill, her father changed her name to Gulabi.

In 2016, Gulabo was bestowed with India's fourth-highest civilian award, Padma Shri for her outstanding contribution in enhancing India's folk-dance culture. Apart from this prestigious award, recognitions and accolades have poured in ever since her first public performance in Pushkar Mela at the age of ten.

'I still remember people clapping in appreciation and astonishment after seeing my first performance. I failed to understand then why they gathered around me and took a few minutes out of their lives to see me, but I felt very special. For the first time, I was not judged for belonging to a lower caste or being a girl. Dance gave me a fresh identity,' she recalls.

From running a dance school in Denmark to expand her legacy internationally, imparting free lessons to girls from rural areas of Rajasthan to soon opening a dance school in Ajmer, Gulabo is going all guns blazing to preserve her dance form.

She takes her passion to grow as a dancer and welcome new developments very seriously. No wonder that, even at forty-nine, she learnt video calling to launch online dance classes. The money she earns is used to support Sapera dancers who are out of work due to the pandemic.

Gulabo's life story is straight out of a film with many highs and lows, and it is her attitude of making the world a better place through her art that is the hero, or rather heroine.

Of Snakes and Dancing

Gulabo's father was out of town when she was born. Upon his return, he learnt about the unfortunate incident of female infanticide, a practice that was prevalent in many parts of Rajasthan a few decades ago.

He called them out for their inhuman treatment of a new-born. Furious with his fight for equality, the village heads ostracized Gulabo's family.

Her father was a *sapera* or snake charmer who would go around the village with a basket of snakes to put up performances that would typically include hypnotizing snakes with an instrument called a *pungi*, juggling, and other acts.

When Gulabo was six months old, her father started taking her along. She would effortlessly tap to the tunes of pungi alongside the snakes and copy their movements. From them, she learnt twirls and flexibility that later became the base of her brand of Sapera dance.

Here's her journey from dancing with snakes to being spotted by Tripti Pandey and Himmat Singh, who worked with the Rajasthan Tourism Department at Pushkar Mela.

Abuse and Applause

In the early 1980s, Gulabo began a new phase of life after moving to Jaipur, one of India's busiest cultural hubs, where people were less conservative. She became a part of the state's cultural and tourism department.

She started working on polishing her dancing skills here. She created her costume of the flowing black *ghagra-choli* and dupatta with decorative laces. The mirror work on the lehenga attracted the attention of the audience.

To ensure that people found this dance easy, she stuck to no rules.

'It is a freestyle dance that heavily depends on fluid body gestures. From snakes, I learnt how to form a U-shape with the body, hip moves, and swirls. It is mainly performed on the beats of the *dafli, manjeera, dholak* and *chang* (types of percussion instruments). There are no prerequisites to this dance. All you need is passion,' she said.

Over the years, she mastered her craft and participated in various functions organized by the government and even got an opportunity to be a part of the government's contingent travelling to Washington D.C. for a show in 1985.

When she returned, most of the regional newspapers had covered the story of a sapera's daughter making India proud in 'Amrika'.

The same people who once humiliated her now welcomed her with open arms, 'Women from our sapera community in Jaipur visited my house and insisted that I teach their daughters this dance. I was also flooded with calls from my native village, and people told me how proud they were. I could not believe that my art form was gradually eliminating the differences,' she recalls.

Performing on the international stage was the turning point in Gulabo's life and there has been no looking back since.

She has a huge fan following across the world. One of the fans is Jyothi Tommaar, who won a National Award for choreographing *Padmavat's* song, 'Ghoomar', in 2019.

'I was mesmerized to see the flexibility and the attitude with which Gulabo danced. Her circles, rhythmic tapping, and costume were very unique. The graceful body movements and her backward arch were unbelievable. Just like snakes, Gulabo does the swinging, flexibility, and hypnotizing circles. While I speak I have visuals in my head of her dancing with her charming smile,' said Jyothi.

Overcoming Challenges

While there was glamour and appreciation, Gulabo's journey has not been without its share of challenges. Even after being a part of so many shows, there are days when Gulabo and artistes like her are out of work. 'As artistes, we do get a lot of respect but we also need money to survive and this is something that the government needs to take care of,' she said.

Jyothi agrees with Gulabo and also highlights the dire need to preserve this art form.

'Late Prime Minister Rajiv Gandhi had started zonal cultural centres, but very little reaches the deserving. With recorded music, TV, films, and so many other available options, we are losing our cultural heritage. The government must do something more constructive. We, as citizens, must respect our culture and should start showing interest in these artforms. I run my academy, the Gangaur Ghoomar Dance Academy, where we invite only authentic folk artistes from Rajasthan to conduct workshops,' she adds.

Gulabo also talks about how the lockdown has further created problems for artistes, 'We have received minimal ration from the government but one dancer has to share it with a family of four or five, which is not enough. No solution that can create an alternate livelihood has been implemented. Dancers like me have the internet so we are managing, but what about those who don't?' Despite such difficulties, Gulabo has managed to stay true to her art while creating her path and carrying forward the legacy. She credits her family members who have stood by her at all times.

'In the initial days, my husband, Sohanath (a classical singer and harmonium player) would visit gymkhanas, offices of private organizers, and event management companies as my agent. His enthusiasm and respect for my work have played an instrumental role in raising awareness about this dance. My children have also learnt this dance and are now teaching others. Finally, I owe everything to my parents who believed I was born to do great things,' said Gulabo.

Whether it was turning abuse into applause, becoming the president of a caste association that once ostracized her for being a girl, or putting the Sapera dance on the world map, this legendary woman's journey is exceptional.

Beating The Odds

Yoshita Rao

Her connection to Mumbai local trains is so innate, one that has seen her through the vicissitudes of life. She started her journey as a beggar, mostly in the ladies' compartment, circumventing the unforgiving glares from men in the general compartment, and now returns as arguably India's first trans freelance photojournalist.

On meeting Zoya Thomas Lobo, you are instantly aware of the confidence she exudes. Her eyes outlined dark with kajal, her shiny golden earrings and thick chain and tiny handbag that matches her outfit shows off her keen fashion sense. And as she begins narrating her story in English, though she fumbles and stammers, one can only admire her fervour for communicating. 'I dropped out of a Convent school in Class 5, but I grew up in a Christian community, so I picked up the language from them,' said the twenty-seven-year-old.

Growing up in Mahim's Kapad Bazar, not too far from the railway lines, with a single mother, who was widowed early on and left to raise two kids, must not have been easy.

'At eleven, I knew I was different from other boys. But I couldn't talk to anyone for fear of being scolded. We used to shift from one area to another area of Mahim, and that's when I met a few friends who I was comfortable enough with to come out to as gay,' said the young photojournalist. 'When I turned seventeen, I met my Guru, Salma, who recognized me as a transgender person. She introduced me to her group, and I felt immediately accepted as one of them,' she added, admitting that she was christened 'Zoya' by her Guru.

A Guru, Zoya explained, is someone who takes you under their wing, almost like a 'motherly figure', who teaches you everything they know about the community, the language and also things like 'how to clap'.

Recalling her first time begging on a train, Zoya says, 'When my [birth] mom came to know that I had joined a group and found a Guru, she was worried that I might fall prey to sex work, but I assured her that I would beg for money and wouldn't sell myself. She travelled with me and observed me the entire time. After that, she was distraught for a whole month, but later, she accepted me.'

'I used to beg for my bread and butter. Trans people do not get a chance to have an occupation. So that was my only source of earning,' she added.

After her mother passed away in 2016, she continued to beg in trains till 2018. 'This pandemic has made me forget my usual train timings,' she laughed, adding, 'During the day, I would roam the ladies' compartments between the stations from Khar to Santacruz, and in the evenings, I would take a train from Bandra to Mahim and Matunga, go back towards Malad and return.' She would be wary of staying back too late or entering the trains too early for fear of the police, who would fine her a sum of Rs 1200. Lunch between train journeys would consist of vada pavs, street carts selling Chinese, and she would treat herself to a 'proper meal' of a thali on better days. She lights up when remembering her earnings during festivals that amount up to Rs 1500, and other days she would earn just Rs 500–800.

Zoya had been begging in the local trains for almost a decade before she got her big break as a recognized photojournalist in 2020, once again while travelling in the local trains. 'My journey as a photojournalist started from the local trains when I was travelling and saw hundreds of migrant labourers protesting outside Bandra station last year. I quickly ran home, got my camera, and clicked those pictures. That's how my pictures were picked up by bigger publications who first heard of my name,' she said.

Views From Behind the Lens

From the crowded lanes of her home in Bandra's Lal Mitti area, Zoya gets up as early as 4 a.m. to take a walk on the sleepy streets of Bandra Reclamation and Bandstand. Whiling away time one day in 2018, watching 'Hijra Shap ki Vardaan Part 1' on YouTube, she pointed out inaccuracies in the comments section, which led her to act in the film's sequel and win an award for her performance too.

'The film industry blatantly casts men and women as transgender people, dressing them in saris, when there are trans people without jobs. The plot then loses its authenticity,' Zoya vehemently states, urging casting directors to turn their gaze towards the community. The rest of her life unfolded smoothly.

The film amassed over 4 million views on YouTube. At an award ceremony for the film, her speech got her noticed by a representative of a local college media agency, who offered her a reporter's job later that year.

'I was a press card holder who didn't know what I needed to do. So I continued to beg on the local trains,' Zoya said, adding, 'The money I earned from begging, I had collected about Rs 30,000 till that point, is what enabled me to buy my first second-hand camera from CST, Bora Bazar [Mumbai],' she said.

Later in 2019, a chance encounter with an experienced photographer set her on the right path. 'My coverage for a "pink" rally, where transgender people were protesting for equal rights, is when I noticed Divyakant Solanki, a senior photojournalist for EPA [European Pressphoto Agency],' she said. It was Divyakant who taught her the nuances of photojournalism.

Her Instagram, with a fan-following of over 1500, is a mix of wildlife photos like monkeys and birds, and more recently, she has showcased poignant photographs depicting life in a pandemic.

Zoya and her elder sister, who were rather close while growing up, fell out when Zoya came out as a trans. 'But now she recognizes my work and is proud of me,' added Zoya. But today, even after receiving her fair share of accolades and recognition, she still resorts to alms from different shops.

Asked if she has plans to go back to school, she says she would if there was a change in the educational system. 'Children don't know what transgender people are. They're only taught about the male and female gender, but there's no discussion about us [trans people],' Zoya said. 'My only hope is that in future trans persons will not be abandoned by their families but loved. This will help in keeping more trans people off the streets.'

This Kerala Trainer is an Inspiration

Serene Sarah Zachariah

Like many girls her age in Mukkam, a remote village in Calicut, Kerala, Jasmine M. Moosa had a fairly uncomplicated childhood. She belonged to a close-knit community, studied in a convent school, and recalls that sipping on ice-candies on the way back home from school was the best part of the day.

But at the age of seventeen, Jasmine's life changed forever.

'I had just returned from school and saw a few visitors at home. My mother asked me to serve them tea. Only after they left did I realize that they had come to ask for my hand in marriage,' said Jasmine.

It was a confusing day, and she repeatedly informed her family that she wasn't ready to get married, but things moved fast. Within a week, she was engaged, and just three days after she turned eighteen, she was married to a man who she met for the first time on their wedding day.

'The night after the wedding, when he walked into the bedroom, I realized that something about his behaviour seemed off. Soon, he tried to pin me down forcefully, and I screamed with all my might. However, in my area, this was considered common. Since many girls were married off at a young age, they assumed it was okay for them to scream on the first night of marriage,' she narrates.

This behaviour continued, and it took a few months for her to uncover the truth: her husband was autistic.

'One year later, I told both families that I wanted a divorce because this was not the relationship I longed for. Eventually, the marriage was called off, but this was hardly the end of my troubles. As soon as I returned home, people started tagging me as the "divorced girl". My family also informed me that I was a burden and that they wanted to get me remarried again as soon as possible,' she explains.

This time, Jasmine made her stand clear and told her father that she wanted to speak with the man before proceeding with the marriage.

'To my surprise, the next alliance that came was exactly the kind of person that I wanted. I openly told him that I was a divorcee, and he assured me that he was ready to accept me for who I was. I was honestly so happy to hear that. I felt like all the dark clouds in my life were moving away and this could be a brand new chapter in my life,' Jasmine said.

She and her family were thrilled.

'I couldn't believe that everything was finally working out for me. But on the night of the wedding, he came into the room and slapped me right across my face. I froze; nothing made any sense. He then tied both my hands and feet, and raped me,' she mentions with a quiet sigh.

The next few months went by in a blur for Jasmine. Her husband, a cocaine addict, would rape her every day and warn her about the consequences of speaking to anyone, even her mother, about this.

So she kept quiet.

'One day, I found out that I was pregnant. It was like a ray of hope for me. I felt like there was a sense of purpose again, a will to live,' she said.

But when Jasmine informed her husband about the baby, he flew into a rage and kicked her in the stomach. She started bleeding profusely and rushed to seek medical help. She also informed her parents about the incident.

'The doctors said that the tube of the uterus had been ruptured and that I would have to undergo surgery to avoid blood loss and to keep the baby alive. I got the surgery, but at five weeks, I lost my baby and soon after, my husband called me to file for a divorce. I was completely dead inside to process any of it. But I had decided that I wouldn't let him get away with what he had done,' she adds.

Jasmine filed a case of domestic violence, and for a while, the police kept trying to settle things between the couple. However, she had voice recordings of the abuse, and they eventually had to arrest him.

'After all this trauma, I wanted to leave the country, but my family was completely against it. They burnt my passport and all my documents, so that I wouldn't be able to go anywhere,' Jasmine said.

This didn't stop her. She fled to Kochi and found a job as a receptionist at a prestigious fitness centre.

'I started building myself up both mentally and physically. The people at the fitness centre gave me all the strength and motivation that I had lacked my entire life. I made a transformation video which went viral, and the encouragement that I received from people who watched it further encouraged me to keep going down this path,' she explains.

Jasmine eventually made her way to Bengaluru. 'I wanted to become a professional fitness trainer, so I came to Bengaluru to do a certification course. At the same time, I worked part-time at restaurants and cafés to sustain myself,' she adds.

Today, Jasmine is a level-three fitness trainer at a reputed centre in Bengaluru.

While Jasmine had a very different idea of what her life would be like, instead of lying down and letting adversity take control, she decided to fight the odds and emerged triumphant. Today, she is a source of inspiration to many young women who are going through similar struggles, and is secure in the knowledge that her inner strength and spirit will help her ride out any storm that life throws her way.

'I have a job, an identity, and people who love and support me every day. If I had waited for things to get fixed on their own, I might not have been alive. But my decision to live my life for myself changed everything,' she concludes with an unmistakable hint of pride.

Section III

Finding Hope

'Hope is being able to see that there is light despite all of the darkness.'

Desmond Tutu

An Agent of Change in Kargil

Rinchen Norbu Wangchuk

For Stanzin Saldon, a thirty-three-year-old social entrepreneur based out of Kargil who also goes by Shifah, conformity was never a strong suit. For as long as Saldon can remember, she always went with her heart and navigated through some rough waters with her independence intact.

She dropped out of medical college to pursue a career in social service. She fell in love, married a man of another faith, and converted to that faith of her own free will despite violent opposition from reactionary elements of the local Buddhist community in Leh. Today, Saldon is actively working for gender equality in Kargil, home to a largely conservative Shia Muslim community, while also improving public school education in this neglected corner of Ladakh.

'Ever since I was a child, I have usually gone with my heart. How I felt about certain situations, my urge to express it, and the spirit of social service are driving factors in everything. In hindsight, it does seem like I overcame difficult and sometimes life-threatening situations. But at the time, it didn't feel that way,' said Saldon, speaking to The Better India.

Today, she runs rZamba, a Kargil-based charitable trust registered in 2017, which is working extensively in education, adolescent health, livelihood generation, and youth leadership. Co-founded alongside her husband, Syed Murtaza Agha, and friends Fayaz Ali, Ali Asgar, and Marzia Bano, rZamba has positively impacted the lives of hundreds of students.

'A woman leading an organization, especially one engaging in social interventions, is quite a new concept in Kargil. In fact, the very idea of a developmental professional engaged in the work I'm doing right now is quite novel here. rZamba means "bridge"' in the Balti language. We are here to act as a bridge between people, resources, systems, and each other,' she added.

Finding her own way

While pursuing her MBBS degree at the Government Medical College in Jammu, Saldon found opportunities to volunteer with a couple of non-governmental organizations (NGOs) working with rural communities in the Jammu area. She had heard about these NGOs during a course in community medicine. Aside from enjoying the course and the experience of working with these NGOs in Jammu, she also realized that her strengths lay in engaging with people, understanding the needs of different communities, and strategizing social programs.

Taking a firm decision, she dropped out of medical college in her second year and enrolled for a bachelor's degree programme in social work through correspondence. It was sometime around the intervening months of 2014 and 2015 when she visited Kargil for the first time in a meaningful way.

She visited with four of her close friends—Murtaza, Fayaz, Ali, and Marzia—from Kargil and began engaging with children, local youth, and their families through various workshops. During these engagements, she began learning more about the region, its myriad challenges, and informally launched rZamba in 2015.

In September 2015, however, she was selected for the American India Foundation's William J. Clinton Fellowship and spent 14 months working with children, especially girl students, studying in government schools across Karnataka. As a Clinton Fellow, she supported government schools by creating learning modules for teachers and students on adolescent health education and building hygienic toilets for girls.

'With my AIF fellowship came some funds, which my friends and I utilized to support the Government Higher Secondary School in Drass. The money was spent on constructing a proper toilet for girls and building awareness among students and teachers about adolescent health and hygiene, particularly periods. While engaging there, we realized the need for a larger overhaul of the public education system in Kargil district. It suffered from inadequate infrastructure and low learning standards among students and teachers. Thus, by June 2017, my friends and I formally registered rZamba to focus on the big picture,' she said.

Between 2016 and 2018, she also worked as a senior programme leader at the New Delhi-based Kaivalya Education Foundation in the erstwhile state of Jammu & Kashmir, where she learned best practices to strengthen public school education.

In the midst of all this, however, Saldon's decision to marry her husband, Murtaza, in 2016 and convert to Islam caused a massive uproar among reactionary elements of Leh's Buddhist community and her family, resulting in the spread of communal tensions in the region.

There were times when the couple had to go underground. They even approached the Jammu & Kashmir High Court to prevent the police in Leh from tracking them down and bringing her back after her parents filed a missing person report.

'I find it very ironic when something like faith, which is supposed to give you courage, strength, and peace manifests in fear, anger, and hatred. Faith is a personal matter to me. Whatever I am today is the by-product of whatever I was in the past. I didn't lose anything in this spiritual realm by converting. Today, I still conform to both Buddhism and Islam. In other words, both philosophies nourish my soul.'

Despite the trauma of undergoing that experience, she continued to soldier on, working with the Kaivalya Education Foundation until 2018. After her stint there ended, rZamba began working with public schools, particularly in Kargil's rural belt. They began conducting baseline assessments of different schools and learning levels of the students in Kargil (2019) to understand the key challenges and issues in the school system.

Working with Kargil

Even today, tourists visiting Ladakh would often stop at Kargil and ask '*Ladakh yahan se kitna dur hai*?' (How far is Ladakh from Kargil?), not knowing that they're already there. It was the Kargil War in 1999 that really brought the region into the national limelight. Developmental works there were largely stimulated by the war and how it was covered by the media, even though it has also borne the brunt of past wars in 1947, 1965, and 1971. Many villages in the Kargil district lie barely a few kilometres away from Pakistan-occupied territory.

Besides geopolitical challenges, the region suffers from roadblocks extending up to six months and poor internet connectivity due to heavy snowfall. Moreover, schools in the region are only functional from March till November, followed by a long winter break. Students in the region, therefore, have a very narrow window of learning.

But what began at the Government Higher Secondary School in Drass with building proper toilets and raising awareness about adolescent health has turned into a full-fledged initiative with a series of government schools in Kargil district, where sixty teachers have undergone intensive workshops and close to 1000 students have benefited directly and indirectly.

'We have encouraged the inclusive engagement of adolescent boys and girls often together in a single room, allowing them to learn about the major changes both genders go through physically and emotionally during this phase of life. As a result, teachers also have experienced a major shift in their relationship with the adolescent kids at their schools, families, and neighbourhoods. In fact, at many locations where girls were shy to express their stories and experiences, their male classmates motivated them to share. Boys also found the spaces safe enough to seek scientific explanations about sensitive topics like masturbation,' claims Saldon.

Kulsum Bano, a Class 10 student studying at the Government Higher Secondary School in Yourbaltak, Kargil, said, 'Thanks to the people at rZamba, a lot of the fears I had in talking about my periods went away. We learnt that getting our periods does not make us dirty. This is a natural process of the human body. Talking about periods shouldn't be taboo, and in society, we need to have more frank discussions about the same. In our society, girls are shy about talking about their periods and relentlessly teased even though it's a natural process. For example, if a girl gets her periods in the playground, I've seen boys laugh behind her back. Today, I'd like to tell these boys to move with the times and change their mindsets.'

Another area of focus has been English language and socio-emotional learning levels. For example, in an assessment that rZamba did with English reading and comprehension for students between Class 9 and 12 (since English is the medium of instruction in most schools in Kargil), they found that 80 per cent were unable even to read a simple single sentence.

'We collaborated with the chief education officer of Kargil, inducted headteachers from sixteen primary and middle schools and trained them on simple yet very effective ways of establishing creative spaces in schools, starting with a school library and assigning reading/storytelling periods to every class. Out of those schools, one primary (Govt. Primary School, Choskore) and two middle schools (in Lobar and Poyen) have been adopted by rZamba to work intensively for three years and support the children with their English and socio-emotional learning,' claims Saldon.

For example, one such project organized for students between the ages of 4 and 8 had them imagine and draw an animal of their choice, and then create a short storybook with their chosen animals. This is a project aimed at boosting their imagination and creativity. It also involves communicating with each other in simple English.

'The baseline assessments and the endline assessments after doing fifteen such projects across different age groups showed immense improvement in the children's learning levels. More than 70 per cent of the children improved by 50 to 60 per cent from their baseline learning levels. Project-based learning not just improves their basic literacy and numeracy but also boosts other soft skills like collaboration, creativity and asking questions, as recorded by our facilitators,' she said.

'Back in late 2019, we invited the rZamba team to our middle school in Choskore Lobar village, where they helped us set up a library. Residents of this area largely come from economically weak and socially backward backgrounds. It's a remote area and difficult for teachers to get here. Internet connectivity is very poor, and online education offers no solution. They don't have the resources to acquire books from outside. Working in close coordination with the students, we created books appropriate for different age groups, like letters of the English alphabet for primary classes. Similarly, for older age groups across five levels, we created age-appropriate books. Before schools closed due to the pandemic, we would allow these children to take the books they co-created back home. We could see a marked improvement in their English language skills each week. This intervention proved invaluable for us teachers as well. If rZamba increases their workforce, they can do real wonders in the entire district,' said Sajjad Ali, who teaches English and Geography.

What they started in 2019 will soon be extended to all schools in Kargil in partnership with the Ladakh Autonomous Hill Development Council, Kargil. rZamba will soon sign an MoU with them. In addition, since July 2020, they have collaborated with the chief education officer and district-level educational institutes to conduct training workshops for teachers and headteachers. They've even collaborated with local, national, and international organizations to ensure quality services.

Muskaan, a student from the Central University in Jammu undergoing a master's programme in Social Work, finished her internship with rZamba as recently as July 2021.

'Saldon has set the standard for every non-profit organization for her collaborative style of management. Her extensive work on the ground to ensure children enhance their learning capacities speaks for itself. While other non-profits are struggling during the pandemic, rZamba continues to make headway into remote communities that don't have access to online learning with their community classes, project-based learning initiatives, and interactive sessions with teachers and parents. What's even more impressive is how they've navigated religious sensitivities nimbly, working closely with local communities,' said Muskaan.

Sustaining Momentum and Covid

The fundamental challenge of every developmental programme is sustaining it. Irrespective of programme design, expertise and external funding, no initiative sustains without engaging local communities and building local resources. This is at the heart of what rZamba does.

Despite successfully carrying out these initiatives, they've had to contend with many roadblocks created by external events like the violent protests in Kashmir in 2016 following the encounter killing of Burhan Wani, a militant. Closer to the Kashmiri populace than their counterparts in Leh, there were definite spillovers of that violent protest in Kargil. Meanwhile, a curfew was imposed in Kargil following protests in the region challenging the abrogation of Article 370 in August 2019, resulting in school shutdowns and restricted movement. And then there is Covid, which has devastated students of this region, who don't have access to adequate internet connectivity.

They organized donation drives for the local administration when medical stocks in hospitals ran low, sanitization drives in villages, and created Covid-related awareness material for local communities. They also joined hands with the District Education Office in Kargil to train teachers individually, to be well prepared once the lockdown was lifted.

'Ladakh also witnessed a reverse migration of professionals and students from different cities to their hometowns and villages. So we decided to leverage their time, skills, and passion for teaching children in their homes. Working with them, we started 'Khangrtsa Yontan', a door-to-door project-based learning initiative through volunteer facilitators. Once the lockdown restrictions were eased a little after the first Covid phase, we also supported community-based classes in collaboration with the Chief Education Office to ensure learning continues even though schools were shut. So far, we have inducted over 200 volunteers in different villages largely in Kargil and engaged more than 3000 school children through project-based learning,' said Saldon.

Looking Ahead

Given how long schools have been shut during the pandemic, there is a clamour among certain education experts for opening schools. In remote corners of Kargil district, where online learning isn't really an option, the need for opening schools is immediate. Of course, this process requires careful calibration, but once it begins, rZamba will continue to make sharper inroads.

'Despite our work so far, it feels like we've just begun. There is still a long way to go,' she said.

Five Years, Five Hundred Reunions

Gopi Karelia

In 2017, Rajesh Kumar, the Assistant Sub-Inspector (ASI) of Panchkula's Anti Human-Trafficking unit, was on his way to Dehradun with a fifteen-year-old boy. He was on a mission to trace the families of such kids, and the fear of breaking this child's heart loomed large in his mind.

Rajesh only had two clues—the boy had somehow been separated from his family in 2007, and his aunt lived in Dehradun. However, he was calm and constantly reassured the boy that everything would be all right.

Upon reaching the city, Rajesh decided that he would not pressure the boy to jog his memory. Instead, the duo walked around the city in the hope that he would remember something, anything familiar. An hour or so later, the boy suddenly remarked that the lane in which his aunt lived had a sewer and a temple. Upon entering one lane with that combination, a girl screamed his name from her rooftop, and later confirmed that the boy was her cousin.

Rajesh verified all the necessary details and found the boy's parents lived in Saharanpur in Uttar Pradesh and handed over the case to the Child Welfare Committee (CWC). A few days later, the parents approached the CWC with the requisite proofs and took their child home.

A major reason why the boy was able to recollect his childhood memories was the protocol followed by Rajesh and his team, which was to build a friendly rapport, gain their trust, but, most importantly, believe them no matter what. Sure, this method took significantly more effort and time—and it could have failed—but that was a risk that the policeman was willing to take.

The teenager is one of the 500 successful child missing cases that Rajesh has solved since his posting as the ASI of the anti-human-trafficking unit in 2015. That year, he solved six cases.

'Helping families reunite after months and years is very emotional and overwhelming for me. On certain occasions, it is very hard to hold back my tears. My father who served in the police force always used to say that let your job set examples of kindness and humanity, go beyond your duty. When I saw the results of sincere effort and time for my first case, I knew I belonged here,' said Rajesh.

The next year, his composure, patience, and alertness helped him solve thirty-three similar cases, and there has been no looking back since. He takes anywhere between an hour to six months to solve one case, but irrespective of the timeline, his commitment and dedication are unshakeable throughout.

Apart from missing kids' cases, Rajesh also works towards rehabilitating beggars and trafficking survivors.

A Multi-Pronged Strategy

Rajesh mentions that being friendly and winning their trust is the key to initiating a conversation with a child who may be coping with the loss of family. 'Once they open up, which may take hours or even months to reveal helpful information, and you have to pay close attention, I usually ask them about their favourite food, family attire, if they remember any shops, rivers or trees. All the kids in Panchkula Child Care Institutions (CCI) may not be from Haryana and I get calls from parents across India for help. In such cases, a child's accent helps in identifying their region,' explains Rajesh.

In certain cases, even one clue from the child is enough to solve the case. Take, for instance, the case of Dimple (name changed to protect identity) from Panipat who ended up in CCI, Shimla, in 2007. She got lost on her way from school and all she vaguely remembered was her dad dealt in carpet weaving.

Using just that one piece of information, Rajesh searched every missing complaint filed by a carpet weaver in Panchkula but in vain. One night it suddenly struck him that Panipat is a hub for carpet-making units. He circulated the girl's photo in police stations and within a few days, her parents identified her.

Rajesh has multiple ways of finding the family. He has formed a WhatsApp group of social workers, CCI members, and police units of various states that look after missing complaints. It has made his work faster. All he has to do is post a picture and details, and he gets a lead and, sometimes, is directly contacted by the family.

Social media, he said, is proving to be a boon. Rajesh also maintains a Facebook page called 'Missing Children Panchkula' where he shares the same details. Other methods include circulating the picture in police stations.

'It is a herculean task to find a child's family that may be living in a different state or has shifted base multiple times.

The WhatsApp group started by Rajesh has eased the channel of communication. We have been able to help a child just by sharing a photograph without any information. His work is always detailed to perfection, and we have been able to solve old cases. Sixty-eight kids living in our shelter house have gotten back with their parents with the help of Rajesh. I remember a couple of cases where he just took a few hours,' said Chandan Singh, child welfare officer, Salaam Baalak Trust (Ghaziabad).

Sushma Kumari from Nari Seva Sadan Mashobra (Shimla) appreciates Rajesh's 'never give up' attitude and said, 'Rajesh has helped us solve cases where we had lost all hope. One child at our shelter was unable to give any information for months. But during a phone call with Rajesh, he ended up naming his school. His warmth and persona are instantly liked by children.'

Follow-ups

After finding the child's family, Rajesh conducts a verification process, before handing over the case to CWC.

'I look through the birth certificate, Aadhaar card, and even conduct a video call with the family if they are in another state, to match the parent's description of the child. On certain occasions where I feel parents are not in a state to support the child, I recommend the CWC to find alternatives or let the child stay at the shelter home. I also have a follow-up system in place to ensure everything is fine by talking to the child. I maintain a personal written record of every case in case anyone wants to take notes,' he said.

Due to follow-up sessions, Rajesh ends up investing extra time in each case. Though his family complains of him attending calls late in the night and visiting other regions without any prior notice, he does not mind.

'On many occasions, I am unable to dedicate time to my own family. They do understand and support my work, but my kids do get sad. Nothing is more important to me than this duty,' he said.

A Woman and Her Dream in the Heart of Sunderbans

Tanaya Singh

'It took me so many years, but I did not give up on my dream,' said Satarupa Majumder, a forty-seven-year-old teacher from Kolkata.

That dream was to take education to one of the remotest areas of the Sundarbans, and it was born in 2012 during her first visit to Hingalganj, an island on the Ichamati River at the Indo-Bangladesh border of West Bengal. For nine years now, Satarupa has been running the Swapnopuron Welfare Society (SWS) in Hingalganj.

Swapnopuron, which means 'a dream come true' in Bengali, is one of the very first English-medium schools in the heart of Sundarbans. With five centres spread across connected islands, Swapnopuron has impacted over 1700 children since its inception.

Satarupa generously carved out some time for me while juggling meetings in Swapnopuron's Kolkata office and planning her trip to the Sundarbans for the weekend. Here's her story of infectious determination, unwavering faith, and tireless hard work.

A Sewing Machine and the Road Trip of a Lifetime

It all started with Satarupa's Toronto-based aunt coming down to India. She had a ritual of making a few donations to help people out during her annual trips. This time around, she asked Satarupa to arrange for a sewing machine to help skill a community of women in the Sundarbans. So Satarupa dug out one of her grandmother's favourite possessions—a Singer machine that had been uselessly lying around ever since she passed away.

Joining her aunt, she took a four-hour-long ride over eighty-six kilometre from Kolkata and reached Katakhali village in Hingalganj. The village mainly comprised families of beedi workers, fishermen, a few farmers, and daily-wage labourers. With the everyday struggles of survival being the focus for residents of the cyclone-prone region, education had taken a backseat.

Satarupa distinctly remembers seeing kids 'who were either playing in the mud or rolling beedis.'

'I couldn't help but compare those kids to my seven-year-old daughter back home. When in preschool, my daughter had access to things like a toddler gym class, a group of peers, and many privileges. In contrast, I was seeing these kids who might never get a chance even to see a decent playground. Could I do something about it?' she said.

The region has several government schools, but the quality of education was dismal, and kids mostly went there just to receive mid-day meals. As a result, many dropped out and got pulled into child labour in the business of making beedis.

Bikash Biswas, a thirty-five-year-old English teacher and branch coordinator with Swapnopuron, said that the area has over twenty government schools. Still, they lack all the required facilities to give these children a safe, nurturing environment.

A resident of Hingalganj, Bikash has a Masters in English Literature and Diploma in Teachers' Education. He completed his education in a government school in Hingalganj itself and went to college and university in Hooghly. The difference between his time at school and government schools in the region now, he said, 'is the way teachers taught. Twenty years ago, the teachers here were motivated. Today, due to poor facilities, lack of infrastructure, and skewed teacher—student ratios—that dedication has dwindled.' (Determined to make a difference, Bikash has been a teacher since 2007. Having begun with the same government school where he was a student, he has now been working with Swapnopuron since 2018.)

Upon Satarupa's arrival in Hingalganj for the first time, few people in the village quickly learnt that she was a teacher. While she had been observing the kids, their parents were observing her. Just before she could leave, they approached and asked her to teach their kids some English.

'I remember casually saying that I would love to come down sometime, but I never really thought I would,' said Satarupa. At the time, she was a middle-school teacher of Economics at a renowned school in Kolkata. On that day in the village, she had a young child back home, a full-time career, a conservative joint family—there was no way she could be back to help.

But, extraordinarily, a few months later, she found herself on a boat ride back to Hingalganj. A firm believer in having a purpose in life, Satarupa said it was the 'call of the universe, and she had to answer it.'

TGIF!

Every Saturday morning, Satarupa would take the 6:20 a.m. local train to Hasnabad station. From there, a rickshaw ride would take her to the Dasha riverbank, followed by a boat ride across the river, and finally an auto-rickshaw ride to Hingalganj. There, she would teach kids till three in the afternoon and make plans for the next week on her way back home.

'I used to do my job at the school five days a week. But I'd always wait for Saturday—a day of all things freedom and happiness. Crossing the river, teaching the kids—it was an adventure for me,' she laughs.

These initial Saturdays involved speaking to parents, counselling those who were not sending their kids to study, gathering kids, and teaching English. In a few months, she had taken eight Katha (0.5 acres) of land on rent using her salary and had set up a makeshift school.

However, getting kids to come regularly was difficult. The area wasn't easy for her to navigate alone. Though she was never scared or doubtful, not knowing anybody in the region was a hindrance. Thus, one of the first stepping stones for Satarupa came in 2014, when she met a man called Aamir Hussain.

Aamir *da*, as she refers to him, was a high school teacher in Basirhat, a town located about thirty kilometre away from Hingalganj. Some people told him about 'this lady who travels every week to teach kids.' Intrigued, he reached out. Impressed by her dedication, he started supporting and encouraging her. He created space for her to work in the community by helping her speak to residents. And when Satarupa decided to hire the first few teachers to join her school, his wife was one of them.

But fate took a sad turn in 2016 when Aamir *da* passed away because of a heart attack. It came as a massive shock for Satarupa. Her strong pillar of support for four long years was no longer by her side.

The Moment of Truth and Triumph

Even in his absence, Aamir *da's* faith was always with Satarupa. Slowly, the work she had been doing started taking roots. Since many of the local teachers she hired didn't have the adequate skills she required, Satarupa arranged for a teacher-training programme at the National Institute of Creative Performance in Kolkata. She also used her salary to pay theirs.

'Convincing them to come to Kolkata once every week was a task in itself. I couldn't have done it without Aamir *da's* support. He helped me convince them by speaking to their husbands and families,' she adds.

Starting with twenty-five kids in Nursery, Lower Kindergarten and Upper Kindergarten classes, Swapnopuron slowly expanded to Grade 4 by 2016. But the moment of truth arrived with the realization that kids were going back to government schools after Grade 4, where the lack of facilities would eventually take them several steps back.

Satarupa knew she had to set up a high school. 'By this time, I had realized that my profession as a teacher in Kolkata alone was not giving me the happiness I sought. So I had to make a concrete decision—either I could continue with my full-time job, or I could set up a high school in Hingalganj.' No prizes here for guessing—she quit her job, along with a very comfortable salary. But the choice came with hesitations about her family's reaction. 'I came from a strict family. Women needed permission to go so far away from home, all alone, and spend that much time at a strange place.'

Moreover, she had a daughter to look after. Thankfully, her husband Debashish Majumder, a businessman in Kolkata, was highly supportive, and her conviction won everyone else's support as well.

Now, she had the fuel she needed to dedicate herself solely to her cause. Using her Provident Fund, Satarupa paid the first advance to lease another piece of land in September 2018, on which she built a structure of hay with ten rooms for Classes 5 to 8. In 2021, Swapnopuron expanded to Class 9. Today, the school charges a small fee of Rs 100–150 per month, which is often waived off for those who can't afford it.

A Steep Climb Up and Up

In 2019, the school grew from 100 to 182 children, and the number kept increasing month on month. Satarupa hired more teachers. Impressed by her work, renowned changemakers in the city joined the organization as board members. Well-wishers pitched in with donations, and her team started raising retail, institutional, and CSR funds.

While following the CBSE curriculum, Swapnopuron focuses on a lot of activity-based learning for primary school. From craft and culture workshops to outdoor activities and storytelling sessions—they focus on the holistic development of children. To conduct such sessions, Satarupa invites experts at regular intervals. They have had people like accomplished storyteller Priyanka Chatterjee and students from Indian Statistical Institute, Kolkata, join them on the island.

The word about their work spread from home to home. Satarupa and her staff members went door to door, convincing parents to send their children to school every year.

In the process, she observed various issues in the community, which involved everything from men abandoning their wives for multiple marriages to children being married off. She felt, first-hand, the insecurities of women and children and resolved to help them.

Working with the West Bengal Commission for Protection of Child Rights, they started conducting several child protection and women empowerment workshops to ensure the schools, families, and society would work together to keep children in classrooms.

Come Cyclones and Viruses; The Dreams Went On

Swapnopuron was among the few educational organizations in the country that could continue teaching despite COVID-19. Satarupa worked with her team to divide students into groups of those who had smartphones at home and those who didn't.

They took a few weeks to prepare and then started online classes. Those with no phones received worksheets in their homes. Additionally, they trained mothers in the area to help kids during online classes. To support the families, the team also distributed 13,550 ration kits over ten months.

Just as the battle against Covid was being won, Cyclone Amphan struck and created havoc in the islands in May 2020. Swapnopuron braced itself again. With Satarupa's encouragement, the team set up six community kitchens and served 76,100 meals over twenty-one days across Hingalganj and five neighbouring islands. They had to stop classes for a month because of the lack of electricity and phone network.

Hearing about their work, people started approaching the organization to help—with funds and volunteers. And together, they began rebuilding projects in the Sundarbans, which included rebuilding houses, cleaning ponds, introducing pisciculture and vegetable gardens as means of livelihood, and several other projects supported by individual donors.

It was this work and their strong reputation that helped Swapnopuron draw the local administration's attention. The administration was amazed to see their progress.

'I have been seeing Swapnopuron's work not only as an educational institution, but also as an organization that is helping empower the local community here. From relief work to empowering women, to bridging the gap in online education during COVID-19, they have done impressive work,' said Sukanta Sarkar, Upa-Prodhan, Hingalganj Panchayat.

The administration reached out to her via the Local Panchayat Sabhapati, Archana Mridha, asking if she would set up centres in other parts of the island. 'I said we definitely would if they helped us with the places to set up centres. So they did, and today we have been able to set up five new centres in six months,' said Satarupa.

Bikash, who was very closely involved in the relief work, calls it one of the most complex and challenging things Swapnopuron has ever done. 'We saw people in the remotest areas lose everything from houses and cattle, to all their belongings, including children's books. Bainara village was one of them. So it meant a great deal to me when we were able to set up a free coaching centre for 205 kids from Bainara for five months after Amphan, followed by a permanent branch near the village,' he said.

One Challenge, One Student, One Teacher at A Time

Towards the end of 2020, Satarupa had started hiring teachers and faculty members from Kolkata and other parts of the country. But human resources, like financial resources, is a huge challenge for the organization. 'Convincing teachers to come to a cyclone-prone area is not an easy task. If I had to hire good teachers, I had to make sure they had a proper place to stay in the Sundarbans,' she said. Satarupa now rents a two-bedroom quarter for teachers to use whenever they stay in the area, and Swapnopuron has a total of sixteen teachers.

Anupa Dutta, an educator with twenty years of experience, is one of them. She quit her job at a renowned school in Kolkata to work with Satarupa. Her role involves everything from teaching to counselling the teachers and parents.

'I live in Hingalganj for 3–4 days a week. My husband and son are not supporting my decision right now, but I have made up my mind,' she narrates excitedly from the teachers' quarter while sharing in the same breath that there's no electricity right now, and she's sweating in the heat. 'When our students are so determined to learn despite all the challenges they face here, why can't we persevere?'

'Education Is Love'

'It's love,' said Satarupa, 'the way every single subject can impact these children.' She tells me about Masoom Birla, the first kid to join her school—who is now in Class 6. Masoom's childhood was scarred with hardships. Coming from an extremely underprivileged background, he has a sick father and an ailing mother at home. But no matter the circumstances, his will to learn drives him and inspires several teachers. 'Masoom was one among the twelve of our students who participated in the Science Olympiad Foundation exam. He won a medal for his performance,' Satarupa shares with pride.

Talking about the impact, Satarupa emphasizes depth over numbers. 'While we began with a small number of kids, we have now seen an urge among the residents to educate their children. Women, who are running their families as single mothers, turn to us for hope today. They approach our teachers and ask for their kids to be educated. This is a tremendous success. Because unless we can impact the entire community in this way, we will not be able to have a long-term impact on the kids.'

Bikash and Anupa agree with this belief. 'Ritika Ghosh, one of my students in Class 1, lost her brother to an accident recently. That little girl was so depressed that she was not able to come to school,' said Bikash, who continued to go to her place to counsel his parents. 'I told them that they had lost their son, but their daughter was there. She would fulfil their dreams. I spoke to them till they were convinced to send her to school,' he said, adding how bright a student she is and how much she loves to dance.

Debjani Adhikari is another such student of Class 3. She lost her father in an accident, and her mother works as a beedi worker. 'Many of these children are first-generation learners. Seeing these parents trying so hard to help their kids get educated always fills me with pride.'

A Dream Come True

Swapnopuron stands true to its name, not only for the students but for everyone involved.

'This place has taught me that nothing is impossible,' said Anupa. She helps me connect with Ruma Das, a resident of Hingalganj who sends her daughters Moumita and Sushmita to the school.

'Compared to the previous Bengali-medium school where my daughters were going, Swapnopuron school has brought a massive change. For me, the biggest change is how they try to talk in English, even at home. English is important for one's career, and I want my kids to learn,' said Ruma. Being a Naik with the Indian Army, Ruma's husband is rarely at home. She manages the house alone while taking care of her in-laws.

Her daughter Moumita, a student of Class 2, one among the thousands for whom these dreams are being woven, chimes in, 'I learn English, Environment Studies, Social Studies, Math, and Bengali at school, and I really like my school. Why? I like my school because it's the most intelligent school. It is an English-medium school,' she said.

Moumita's smile is a testament to the fact that though it took many years, Satarupa Majumder never gave up on her dream.

India's Glass Woman

Gopi Karelia

The universe took nine months to craft me,
Yet, it wasn't enough for my bones to be crafted to perfection

—*Dhanya Ravi*

At first glance, you might sympathize, feel sorry or wonder what is up with the girl in the wheelchair. But her childlike smile with a hint of quirkiness will push you to know more about her. Once you to break the ice, her intriguing words, sharp wit, and chirpy attitude will bowl you over.

While conversing, do not panic if she breaks a bone upon sneezing, as this is what she calls 'another day of life'.

Meet Dhanya Ravi, fondly known as 'India's Glasswoman' from Kerala now settled in Bengaluru. Twenty-nine-year-old Dhanya suffers from Osteogenesis Imperfecta (OI), also known as brittle-bone disease. It is a rare genetic disorder that mainly affects the bones making them brittle and prone to easy breakage. Dhanya was born in the winter of 1989, in a family that eagerly awaited a girl child. Her parents Ravi and

Nirmala were overjoyed but underlying the happiness was a thread of worry over the constant crying and health issues of the new-born.

Dhanya was only fifty–six days old when her thigh bone broke. It was then that medical experts identified the symptoms of the rare disease in the' new-born. The doctors had to relay to them the sad news of their daughter having been born with OI. They also informed Ravi and Nirmala that as OI is incurable, Dhanya's life would not be like that of another child. To provide Dhanya the best medical care, her parents travelled across India but with no tangible results.

'Like every parent, we wanted nothing less than the best for our daughter. But wherever we went, the doctors told us that her survival is a miracle. Many hospitals shut their doors. In times like these, the doctors are supposed to give counselling and help the patients and their family,' said Ravi.

Each day, there was new learning for Ravi and Nirmala. When Dhanya became old enough to understand the precarious situation of her body, her parents, instead of restraining her in overprotective bonds and suffocating her childhood, allowed her to grow wings and fly solo whenever and wherever she could.

'I was around five years old when I understood what is OI. In very simple terms, I was told that my bones would break for no reason. I was mentally prepared to lead to a different childhood but every time a bone would break, I would be clouded by gloominess. With persistent support from my parents and brother Rajesh, I'm still finding possibilities to overcome my challenges.' Even though Dhanya was given the freedom to think for herself and make her own decisions from a very young age, the environment and mindset prevailing in the society served as a reminder that she is a different child.

At an age where other children would be busy buying toys, Dhanya was busy selecting her wheelchair. There were times when people would come up to a fourteen-year-old Dhanya and ask the reason behind her appearance. Instead of feeling sorry for herself or being embarrassed, the teenager would calmly explain her condition with patience.

'Till date, people look at me as if I am an alien. Because there is a lack of awareness about rare diseases and sensitivity around the subject, people stare, and some even pass comments. My parents are bothered by it, but I tell them their daughter is a celebrity,' she said in a telephonic interview from her brother's house in Boston, United States.

Forbearance, being her one true virtue, Dhanya suppressed her desires to do everything a kid her age was doing, 'It was tough seeing the kids in my building play and run around with so much ease.'

Dhanya, however, is grateful to her elder brother Rajesh who made sure that the spirit of sibling rivalry was always present in the house. From fighting over the TV remote to awaiting their favourite 'Mango' season, they were each other's biggest supporters and critics.

While she tried to do the most basic things in her daily life, hospitals remained a constant throughout her childhood and now, 'There are more fractures in my body than wounds. Due to dental and eye deformities or respiratory issues, I became very familiar with hospitals at a very young age, and soon they became my second home.'

Once in two weeks, a bone would break, and due to this severe health risk, many schools in Bengaluru turned

Dhanya away. So, she chose the next best thing to mainstream schools—home—and completed her high school with home tutoring. Dhanya owes her educational life, knowledge and her love for writing to Victoria, her neighbour, who spent an hour every day with her for almost ten years, 'Victoria aunty is the epitome of selfless love. She didn't even take a penny for tutoring and mentoring me. More than textbook chapters, I learnt life lessons from her.' Victoria's constant motivation and support from friends to pursue higher education helped Dhanya clear a preparatory course from Indira Gandhi National Open University (IGNOU). She also completed an Online Novel Writing certificate course.

To sum it up, Dhanya's childhood was different but a happy one. For her, seeing her parents cry every time she is rushed to the hospital or her refraining from eating cake fearing her teeth breaking, was more heartbreaking and painful than having her bones break.

Every part of her body has been through excruciating pain many times, and there is no way to know or prepare for the next episode. Every time a bone breaks, her mobility in the affected area is restricted, 'Thank god my tongue doesn't have any bone,' she chuckled.

Opening Pandora's Box

Life took a dramatic turn when Dhanya discovered another side of life that was sans any dependency, weakness, or pain.

It was coming across classical music, the world of cinemas and novels. Since Dhanya was confined to the four walls of her bedroom, she grew up listening to the music of the likes of composer and singer A.R. Rahman, K.J. Yesudas, and

Raveendran Master, a popular South Indian music composer and playback singer from Kerala. 'I am very fond of music as it helps me heal every time I am down.'

An avid reader, fiction is her favourite genre and authors like Preethi Shenoy and Dr Paul Kalanithi are the reason behind her penchant for writing.

Internet is another source that helped her build an active social life and connect with like-minded people, 'Computer opened a plethora of doors that helped me become the person I am today.'

Today, Dhanya maintains a personal blog 'Dhanya Ravi— Where words speak' and she is also working as a freelance columnist and web content writer. She regularly updates her blogs with her personal experiences and quotes penned by her to help people like her overcome challenges.

'I was born rare, will die rare, and I will remain rare,' reads one of the quotes.

She started reaching out to people living with OI or with other rare conditions. This evolved her as a person and also made her more aware. It was through the power of the internet that she came across Binu who lives with OI. When Dhanya reached out to her readers and friends to raise funds for his surgery, she received a tremendous response. Dhanya and her online friends were able to aid Binu. After surgery, he now works as an assistant in a Kochi hospital. Post this incident, Dhanya made it her mission to create awareness and sensitize people about rare diseases.

'I want to educate people about inclusion and acceptance, and empower people with disabilities. Even now there are stigmas in the society and parents are often ashamed to take their child with deformities out. Many parents are not fully informed about the way they should handle such kids,' she said.

Though the situation has improved, there is still ignorance and lack of proper healthcare facilities, 'Presently, there are very few healthcare facilities in India that are equipped with a rare disease cell. If enough education and counselling are given to people, then such diseases can be prevented with the right precautions.'

Echoing her sentiments, Dhanya's physician Dr Sunitha said, 'Routine screening and genetic abnormality tests and awareness about it should be given more priority. Not everyone is as strong as Dhanya is.'

For the last couple of years, she has been associated with several NGOs that work towards the same cause. From speaking at events like marathons, TEDx Talks to delivering motivational talks in educational institutes, Dhanya is doing everything in her capacity to reach out to the maximum number of people.

Such events have also increased her social circle, and now she has several friends who understand her situation and are always there for her. One such friend is Namitha Kumari, a thalassemia patient. Namitha recently launched her website Open Platform for Rare Disease (OPFORD). It is a digital platform to connect rare disease patient communities, parents and caregivers to improve diagnosis, treatment, and care of rare diseases. Dhanya, along with her peers, is helping out Namitha spread awareness about the website. 'There are no barriers in our friendship despite our limitations. We help each overcome our own issues, and I am blessed to have her in my life,' said Namitha.

Arjun Som, a life and relationship coach, is Dhanya's friend and is also a silent supporter who is only a phone call away, 'Dhanya is so full of life that it is challenging to not be friends with her. Her adorable and warm smile will make anyone comfortable. We have conducted several awareness drives together and will continue to do so in future.'

Dhanya received the National Award 2018 in the Role Model category by the Department of Empowerment of Persons with Disabilities India for her activism. She is also a recipient of 'Brave Bangle Award 2012' and 'Annual Inspired Indian Foundation (IIF) Award 2014.'

When Disability is Just Another Word

Currently, Dhanya is visiting her brother in Boston despite knowing the risks of travelling across continents. She left India in January, and so far, has managed to tick off a couple of things from her bucket list. From going to New York to see the Statue of Liberty to spending time on the beaches of Miami, Dhanya is shattering all the myths and limitations that are tagged with the disabled.

She is also actively spreading awareness in America about rare diseases. A few weeks ago, she was a part of a fundraising event in Boston where she helped an NGO from Kerala, 'People are the same everywhere, and even here ignorance regarding rare diseases is rampant.'

Strange looks from people in foreign countries have not deterred Dhanya's quirky humour. When a local asked Dhanya where her legs were, she said, 'My legs are very much here, just that they are not as tall as yours.'

For Dhanya, her disability has unlocked the tremendous potential inside her, 'My disability taught me that nothing could scar my confidence as long as I choose to keep my face towards possibilities. There is always a hidden blessing beneath adversity.'

Her only appeal to the parents of children with or without disabilities is identifying the potential of their kid and nurturing it with care. 'Every child is blessed with skills and honing it is the parent's duty. Give your child education and let him/her explore social life. This will help them become a better person each day.'

Dhanya is grateful to her parents and brother, who believed in her and remained a source of strength at every step. She is thankful to her childhood friends who did not treat her any different and stuck with her throughout. As she counts and appreciates the number of blessings in her life, her nephew is waiting impatiently to show her his new PlayStation. She has a busy schedule ahead and come evening, she has to attend a social gathering.

Nothing has changed for Dhanya, and yet every day is a new day for her that she embraces with excitement and a little bit of nervousness. Dhanya's chirpiness, her undying spirit, optimism for life, and droll humour have not only encharmed but has also inspired me.

His Biryani Took Off!

Yoshita Rao

How good do you think your home-cooked biryani recipes are? Well, a newly minted home chef from Dehradun gets calls from celebrities such as Swara Bhaskar and Mrunal Thakur, some of whom have even made the trip to the city—just for a serving of his delicious Yakhni Pulao and creamy Chicken Korma.

On any given Sunday, Sameer Sewak is up at 5 a.m. to prepare at least sixty kebabs, twenty kilos of biryani, and five kilos of butter chicken. As he lives on the edge of Dehradun, on the way to Mussoorie, he said, 'People passing through to get to Mussoorie stop over to order or people who have summer homes here also order from me.' Sameer takes a maximum of twenty orders on weekends and makes around Rs 20,000.

Interestingly, Sameer didn't plan on being a chef. He wanted to be a pilot. 'I grew up next to the airport in Agra, and while I spent a major chunk of my childhood there, I also spent some time in Nainital. My grandfather was in the air force and that rubbed off on me a little bit,' said Sameer, who went on to do his pilot training after completing Class 12.

But it was not too long before he made a life-changing decision to trade in his wings for a *chulha* and a few big *degchis* (copper vessels, often used to cook biryani).

Taking Off as a Biryani Chef

'When I was about to join the industry, it was probably the worst time to be a pilot in three decades,' Sameer said, in reference to airlines like Kingfisher Airlines and Jet Airways shutting down. 'There was a huge line of pilots, who already had the experience, waiting for employment. And with COVID-19, more pilots lost their job,' he said, adding that his career as a pilot never got a chance to take off.

For four years from 2008 till 2012, Sameer underwent pilot training at the Prairie School of Mission Aviation in Canada. On returning to India the following year, he couldn't convert his Canadian licence for use in India, as he couldn't complete his requisite hours of training.

'There's a lot of bureaucracy and red-tapism when it comes to pilot training in India. To convert your licence here, you have to pass a lot of exams. If you want to be employed by a particular airline, you have to pay for your own training on the aircraft, which could go up to Rs 15 lakh for a two-month course. They also kept saying that I needed to complete my training in Canada,' he said.

While waiting for his big break as a pilot, Sameer dabbled in digital marketing for a few brands and also worked as a research assistant. 'I was supposed to do my training as a flight instructor in Canada in the summer of 2020 but then COVID-19 happened,' he laughs, admitting that as fate would have it, he always came back to his other passion—cooking.

'I cooked a lot in between, even in Canada, to sustain myself. I had a string of odd jobs like working at a petrol station and in a Mexican grill as a cook. Or I cooked simply because I missed Indian food,' said the thirty-year-old.

His love for food, especially Lucknowi cuisine, stems from memories of his grandmother cooking on a chulha. 'At big family get-togethers, my grandmother used to cook on the chulha. Due to the pandemic, when we couldn't get out, this was a fun thing to do as a family,' said Sameer, whose Instagram account is filled with pictures of him cooking amidst a breathtaking view of the Dehradun hills.

The Boy from the Hills

After experimenting with just two dishes—chicken korma and biryani, and receiving enough encouragement from his friends and family, Sameer decided to start a catering business on the weekends in September 2020.

Now, every Thursday, he uploads a new menu to add to his Awadhi flavoured-dishes like methi malai paneer, dal bukhara, butter chicken, mutton shami kebabs, and baingan ka bharta, among others. The chulha expert's cooking venture took off in a big way and how. 'Now I have people coming from Mumbai, Bengaluru, and Delhi for my food,' he said, including the outpouring of requests he gets from Dehradun. Recently, he even catered for an in-flight crew. The meal, of mutton and kaale chane ke shami kebab burgers, was for a Mumbai–Dehradun flight.

But his most surprising customer, till date, was *Veere Di Wedding* (2018) actor Swara Bhaskar. 'Swara posted a picture of Mussoorie on social media and I know the area pretty well.

So, I tweeted to her saying, "I know this is a long shot but just in case you're craving some chicken biryani and korma up in the mountains . . . I'll come up and deliver it to you,'" Sameer said, adding that he was stoked when she got in touch for an order.

'She was kind enough to post it on her social media,' he adds.

Swara vouched for his biryani and korma on her Twitter and Instagram handles. 'A #twitter short story with a yummy happy ending! @sameersewak I cannot thank you enough for your generosity, effort and thoughtfulness. I deeply I appreciate ur gesture. It feels like there is hope in the world when strangers are so kind. thank u! And the Food was DELICIOUS . . . (sic),' she tweeted.

Sameer was later approached by *Batla House* (2019) actor Mrunal Thakur who was in town for a shoot, playback singer Ankur Tiwari who was also in Dehradun, writer Snigdha Poonam, who also took a portion of Yakhni Pulav for her husband in Delhi, and Mariellen Ward, an award-winning Canadian blogger.

To Cook on a Chulha

Currently cooking Lucknowi cuisine up in the mountains from his own backyard, Sameer said his Yakhni pulav is a replica of his grandmother's recipe. Having learnt the dish from his mother, Swapna, who learnt it from his grandmother, Sameer said, 'My grandma was from Lucknow and Yakhni pulav was her signature dish. It is revered among the Muslim community, and in Bareli, Allahabad, and even in Pakistan. The other dishes are just my take on Lucknowi cuisine.'

Speaking of his love for cooking on the chulha, Sameer said, 'The food flavour hits differently,' adding, "My grandma used to cook with a lot of passion and I used to learn just by watching her cook. But it takes a lot of work to cook on a chulha, and that is how she wanted to prepare food on special occasions. The high flame from the burning firewood, the coal—all contribute to unique flavours.'

Cooking up a storm in the mountains requires one to constantly monitor the flame, which is no mean feat.

To set up a makeshift chulha you need mud or bricks, firewood, coals, and a fan to intensify the flame. 'Biryani, pulav, and korma cook better on intense heat,' said Sameer, who bought a battery-operated fan to control the flame.

To cater to all-time favourites, Sameer invested in a commercial freezer along with up to 50-kilo deghchis. And while he used to get stressed about the consistency of taste when cooking larger quantities, he has become more organized. 'I went from cooking 5 kilo of biryani to 20 kilo, but the taste has been consistent.'

Na Cheez Foods

'My venture has picked up enough for me to open a bigger kitchen. I have rented out another space with a nice backyard and I am currently interviewing chefs and kitchen staff to be a functioning daily kitchen instead of taking orders only on weekends,' Sameer said, adding that he wanted to open by January 2021. 'But the hiring phase is a big task as I am very particular about how the dishes need to be cooked. There should not be any dilution of the recipe,' he adds.

While the second wave of COVID put a spanner in his plans he is still hopeful to open 'Na Cheez'—from the Urdu phrase, which is also his Twitter handle (@naa_cheese).

Sameer doesn't fail to mention that this wouldn't have been possible without the help of his family who initially helped him out with his bulk orders. His mother helped with the food prep, his father taught him how to set up the chulha, and his little sister, Ria, helped him get organized with the orders by preparing spreadsheets. He regularly takes his dog Lisa, who is 'the happiest' in his family about his cooking venture, on grocery shopping trips as well.

'It brings me great joy and pride that the food we love in our family is being loved by so many people,' said Sameer's father Regginald.

Finding Art in the Discarded

Vidya Raja

What would you do with a few bottle caps? Throw them away? But thirty-nine-year-old Harminder Singh Boparai uses such discarded pieces to create stunning works of art.

His latest work, titled *Life*, consists of discarded bottle caps, which he has used to make a fish sculpture.

What's unique is how each piece of art he has created has an inspiration and a story behind it. His sculptures seamlessly integrate modern and traditional ideas.

Harminder crafts his works of art from scrap metal and discarded materials, and has won many national and international accolades and awards for his work. Being left partially paralysed at the age of eleven did not deter his artistic creativity in any way. If anything, he only worked harder to carve a niche for himself.

Is Academic Excellence the Be All and End All?

Born in Ghudani Kalan, a village in Punjab, Harminder said that while he was always inclined towards the arts, he was never a very bright student. 'In hindsight, I can say that it does not matter, but it was tough when I was in school and a below average performer,' he said. He describes himself as a 'backbencher' when it concerned academics, but always grabbed the first spot when it came to any art competition.

Recalling one such competition, he said, 'When I was in Class 7, we were asked to make a sculpture from home and present it for the competition at school. I made a sculpture of Mahatma Buddha and that was the first time I saw my parents being proud of me.'

However, his artistic skills didn't impress people around him and Harminder speaks about how he was often referred to as 'trash'—only because he wasn't doing well academically. It was also around this time that Harminder had a stroke attack, which left his right side paralysed.

'It took me close to three years to regain some of the strength in my right side and because of that I further deteriorated in my academics,' he said. Harminder would often hear people taunt and speak about what he would do in life given his physical condition. 'The situation is so different today. Schools are willing to look for aspects that children are good at other than academics. When I was growing up, I had no such luck,' he said.

Harminder speaks of the undue pressure put on him to excel in academics, and said, 'It was not like I did not want to do well, but I could not study. That was not what I was meant to excel in. Looking back, I can say that it was difficult.'

'For all the hardships I encountered, my life now is filled with contentment.'

Despite a rather difficult and turbulent childhood, there is not an ounce of anger or sense of defeat in Harminder's voice. Instead, he said, 'I grew up in a time when academics was important. No one even thought that I could make a name for myself in the arts. I cannot blame anyone, all they were doing was look out for me.' He compares his life to that of an unpolished diamond, and how it goes through severe hardships before actually being recognized as a worthy stone.

There are far too many difficulties that Harminder encountered while growing up. From losing his older brother in 1992 to having to work very hard to make ends meet as a family. 'My parents had to worry about marrying off my five older sisters. I understand why they were sometimes hard and harsh on me,' he said.

It was during one of the classes that his teacher Manoneet Kalsi noticed Harminder sitting and drawing. She saw potential in his work and pushed him to participate in the college cultural festival. 'That was the starting point for me. She took me to the arts department and literally started me off on my journey,' he said.

From Punjab to Michigan

From being unsure of participating in competitions to winning the Gold Medal at the Zonal Clay Modelling Competition for three consecutive times from 2002, Harminder found his true calling in a Punjab college. From there he enrolled at the TAC Academy of Fine Arts, Ludhiana, in 2003 and pursued a two-year diploma in sculpture-making. With time, his work started getting recognition and in 2007, his work was displayed at the India Academy of Fine Arts.

Yet another turning point in his life came in 2015 when he visited the US where his sisters were living. 'I encountered a completely different way of life and learning in the US, and that has also contributed to shaping the person I am today,' he shares. In Punjab, where his initiation into the world of art started, he said, no one even knew what sculpting and clay modelling were. Whatever he learnt was on his own there.

A solo exhibition sponsored by the Holland Arts Council further helped Harminder grow as an artist.

Being at the centre, he was able to display his work in countries like Germany, United Kingdom, Italy, and Brazil. There, he became known for working with what is conventionally called 'trash' and turning them into pieces of art. 'I started by just picking up some discarded wooden golf clubs from a local scrap dealer and found ways to turn them into art. Scouting for scrap and visiting local garage sales became my thing,' he said, with a hearty laugh.

From showcasing his work at the Van Singel Fine Arts Center in December 2016 to being selected in the Top 100 ArtPrize 2016—which attracts more than 1500 artists from across the globe—he has done it all. Closer home, Harminder bagged the Lalit Kala Punjab award in 2012 and the National Art Ikon Award from HammerArt in 2013.

While he is an artist par excellence, his grit and never-say-die attitude is also worthy of commendation.

Section IV

On Loss

'Death is not the opposite of life,
but a part of it.'

Haruki Murakami

'Did I Not See the Signs?'

Vidya Raja

It only takes a few minutes for your life to do a complete 180-degree turn, and no one can understand and relate to this sentiment better than me, Raashi Thakran. On 6 January 2019, my younger brother, who was all of eighteen, died by suicide. Life, as I knew it, has not been the same since then.

At 8.45 p.m. on what I can only describe as a regular evening at home, the doorbell rang and before I could process what was happening, my father, Rajeev Thakran, ran out of the house.

I only vaguely heard what he mumbled on his way out. I called him a few seconds later on his mobile, and all I heard was a cry. I remember being gripped by a fear that I can never put in words.

Until that moment, I had never imagined that my father could cry. All he said was, 'Raghav is gone.'

'Raghav Was a Joy to be Around'

Raghav was three years younger than me. Like most other sibling relationships, ours was fraught with fights, arguments, bickering, and a lot of love.

I would very often tease and irritate him, so much so that people often mistook me to be the younger one.

While twenty months have passed by since that night, the hurt, guilt, anger, and pain lingers on.

Raghav was always quite mature for his age. He was an extremely sensitive soul and would always take time to open up. But once he did, he was a joy to be around.

I miss him, and no matter how many times I say these words, the pain refuses to leave me. Raghav was the kind of boy who would find beauty in pretty much everything— sunsets, butterflies, rain, the stars. He sought out the good in people and things around him.

Raghav was my confidant and my ally in the truest sense. He rooted the loudest for me and believed in the dreams I had. I still cannot believe I lost him to suicide.

Did I Not See the Signs?'

I often ask myself—did I miss something? Could I have helped? I don't have the answers. And I doubt I will find them.

Raghav was always happy. In hindsight, maybe a little too happy. We would discuss a whole range of things, from celebrity suicides to mental-health initiatives. But I don't know why we never asked each how we were feeling.

Should I have dug a little deeper?

I thought I knew him. I thought if he ever had a problem, I would be the first person to whom he reached out.

I misread him.

My idea about the relationship I shared with him changed after his suicide, and I am now left feeling that perhaps I didn't know him as well as I thought I did. That is what stings.

'Ask, Don't Wait for the Other Person to Speak'

Raghav would always enquire about my college, how I was faring, etc., and we would speak about things that seemed to trouble him at school as well.

I assumed he would come and speak to me about things that troubled him. I never explicitly asked him any questions, and he never confided in me.

The guilt of not asking him is something I carry within.

Immediately after the suicide, I spent many months feeling incredibly guilty. Even now, I am not entirely sure I want the feeling to go away. I think I will live with the guilt.

I feel so pissed with myself. Perhaps I was so caught up in my dreams that I lost track of Raghav's feelings and insecurities. I didn't take a step back and check in on him as I should have. I feel like I was so short-sighted and selfish that I didn't watch out for my baby brother.

There was a phase after his death, where I would wake up because of nightmares; the anxiety and guilt almost started hurting me physically. I had to seek medical intervention and take prescribed medicines to be able to function normally again. It's a very crippling feeling—the loss of a loved one, to suicide.

Couldn't Help Raghav but Need to Help Others

Raghav's suicide brought mom, dad, and me closer. We wallowed in our collective loss and found solace in each other. There are days when dad and I are okay, and mom is in a terrible state, so we help her through it and on other days I am down in the dumps. It's a cycle, and each day brings new emotions, and we are all learning to deal with our collective loss.

To those who are left behind, life is never the same again. And my way of dealing with the pain was also to immerse myself in work—petitioning the government to set up a 24/7 suicide helpline.

I remember desperately calling some of the suicide helplines listed on Google only to find them all not functioning. That broke my heart.

What if Raghav had tried one of those numbers just before the suicide? Maybe if he had spoken to someone, he would have changed his mind.

It's over for Raghav and nothing I do or say will ever get him back, but I can try and help others who might be in a similar situation.

Channeling Loss into Compassion

Ananya Barua

Lalmati and Mohanlal were over the moon. After trying and waiting for seventeen long years, they were finally going to be parents. But the joy was short-lived, as their son, Shiv, was born twelve weeks premature, and his weight was only one kilogram.

Although he was being treated in a Level III intensive care unit and was under constant vigilance, he kept losing weight, and after twenty-three days, he was diagnosed with Patent Ductus Arteriosus (PDA), a heart disorder.

PDA occurs when there is an' unwanted connection between the two major blood vessels of the heart—the aorta and the pulmonary artery. Because of this condition, children face various health problems that not only impede growth but also create more complications.

Mohanlal, a labourer, was not in the position to afford the new-born intensive care unit (NICU) care at the government hospital, and seeking tertiary paediatric care in a private hospital was out of the question.

In this moment of darkness, this family finally found some light when the Genesis Foundation, a Gurugram-based

NGO which provides medical support to children with heart problems, especially Congenital Heart Disease (CHD), came to their rescue.

With its help and support, a team of doctors performed a historic surgery, called PDA device closure, in Thane's Jupiter Hospital. After eighteen hours of surgery, Shiv was finally safe.

Nothing short of a miracle for his parents and a landmark for the medical fraternity, Shiv became the smallest baby in India to undergo the procedure.

Today, Shiv is among the 3200 children across the country who have benefitted from the Genesis Foundation.

CHD affects more than two lakh children a year, with one-fifth of them requiring intervention in the first year after birth. In other words, as per the report of Indian Academy of Paediatrics (IAP), nine out of 1000 children in India are born with CHD.

And despite its prevalence among all economic sections of the society, the lack of awareness and cost of treatment results in children being denied the opportunity to survive and recover.

Genesis Foundation wants to bridge this gap.

The co-founder of the foundation, Jyoti Sagar said, 'Even though cardiac treatment and care is very advanced in India, more than 80,000 children are suffering from CHD every year. Costing around Rs 1–6 lakh, the treatment and surgery are often not affordable for many. So we step up to help any such family with a monthly income of less than Rs 15,000.'

A Personal Loss to Mass Change

The origin of the NGO comes from a place of personal loss for the founders, Jyoti and Prema Sagar. Back in 1983, the couple had lost their second child to the same disease, only twenty-four hours after he was born. They had named him Sameer.

'The agony and pain of losing a child is unimaginable. When this had happened to us, there wasn't much awareness about it nor was the treatment as advanced as it is today,' said Jyoti.

Devastated, the two began their search for purpose, a way that could help them endure the pain of such a huge loss. In 1984, they came across Missionaries of Charity, an international organization working for the poor, and began volunteering for various social-work initiatives.

'During this time, we slowly realized the seriousness of congenital heart disease and how frequent it was. We didn't want any other parent to have to go through that, especially due to financial constraints. The idea of doing something in this area came to us, and we started the foundation,' adds Prema.

While in the initial years Genesis focussed on various chronic illnesses such as cancer, thalassemia, and cardiovascular issues, they eventually narrowed it down to congenital heart ailments in 2017.

Hospitals like Columbia Asia in Bengaluru, Jaypee Hospital in Noida, Amrita Institute of Medical Sciences and Research Centre in Kochi, MIOT Hospital in Chennai, Jupiter Hospital in Mumbai, etc., now work in association with the foundation, by informing the NGO's social service cells and administrative units whenever a case of an underprivileged child with CHD comes through their doors.

To make sure the funds go where they are needed, the foundation first reviews the family background and income certificate of parents before sponsoring the treatment costs.

'With a core team of seven members supported by hundreds of volunteers, the foundation has been running a robust network to combat CHD. Our programme goes much beyond writing a cheque. The foundation not only funds treatment and surgery but also continues to help with follow-ups and aid through any post-op needs regularly. For instance, Shiv continues to receive periodic check-ups and is in a good condition, weighing around five kilograms now,' he adds.

Through various fundraising events and awareness drives, the foundation is trying to tackle the issue from the root.

'Firstly, it is important to have an understanding of how grave the problem is. CHD is the second highest cause of infant mortality in the world, irrespective of geography or economic conditions. Unless there is proper awareness and timely intervention, most of these children might not even reach their first birthday. The second most important aspect is correct diagnosis. A thorough check-up of the new-born allows one to identify any major issues of concern at an early stage to initiate adequate treatment,' he said.

After having put forth a consolidated effort in the area for all these years, Genesis has emerged to be one of the largest NGOs working in this space.

'However, there is still a long way to go. We don't have a numerical goal for impact because at the end of the day saving even a single life is a huge step towards a better and safer world for our children. I hope that our work ensures that certainty and safety for future generations,' concludes Jyoti.

The First Born

Rinchen Norbu Wanghuk

It was just another pleasant summer day in July 2015. I, Rinchen Norbu Wanghuk, was in Leh, and as always, my aunt and I were having a wide-ranging conversation on various issues of the day.

However, there came a moment when she told me something that left me flabbergasted. My mother, Rinchen Wangmo, had a child before me, who died just days after he was born.

My reaction to the news was one of shock, sadness, love, and empathy for my mother. But I had so many questions in my mind. Why hadn't she told me about my brother? What really happened? How did my parents cope with the pain of losing a child?

For years, these questions were always at the back of my mind, but I neither found the opportune moment or the courage to bring up this tragic episode. Moving to Bengaluru in the winter of 2017 further robbed me of the chance to ask these questions. Finally, I mustered the courage to first ask my father, Sonam Wangchuk, about this episode earlier this week (February 2020).

Strangely enough, there wasn't even a hint of awkwardness in our conversation. My father was kind enough to reopen an episode he had left far behind and went into some detail about what had happened.

However, what that conversation did was give me the courage to ask my mother directly. And once again, without a hint of awkwardness or annoyance, she told me her story.

Early Days

My parents had an arranged marriage in December 1986 in Leh. When they got married, they knew each other, although there was little they knew about each other.

At the time my father was working as private secretary to the two-time Member of Parliament of Ladakh, the nineteenth Bakula Rinpoche, who at the time was a member of the National Minorities Commission.

After their wedding, my parents left Leh for Delhi where Rinpoche was working. My parents were living in Delhi, away from the support and guidance of their family. Within months of their marriage, my mother was pregnant with her first child.

At the time, my mother was only twenty-three years old, while my father was approaching thirty-one. Back home, people had greeted the news with a lot of happiness, and preparations for the incoming baby began in earnest. Clothes and a crib were bought, while my aunts and grandmothers began knitting baby socks and sweaters.

'But during my fifth or sixth month of pregnancy, I had noticed that there was barely any foetal movement. Earlier, I had accompanied your father for a visit to Varanasi, where

I suffered a serious bout of diarrhoea. Forced to return to Delhi, I immediately went to my doctor, who took care of the problem, or so it seemed. She had told us that everything was normal,' she recalls.

Losing a Child

But in the following weeks, she began to lose a lot of weight. By the time she was eight months pregnant, a very critical time, her doctor had realized that something was wrong, but she had no remedy at hand.

'For the longest time I had told my doctor that something was wrong, but she kept assuring me, everything was all right. Upon seeing my condition, she immediately referred me to the nearby Batra Hospital. After a full check-up, the doctors there told us that the heartbeat of the foetus was very low, and there was no option but to conduct an emergency Caesarean surgery. My firstborn son was born in the first week of February 1988, but died days later because of serious heart complications,' recalls my mother.

It was a devastating loss, and it had a serious impact on my mother's physical and mental wellbeing. Some of my family members and relatives consoled her by saying that had the baby lived he would have suffered further health complications down the line. There was nothing she could do about the situation, they said.

But that's a small consolation because the loss was real.

However, it was also an incredibly busy time at the family home in Delhi with my granduncle, the nineteenth Bakula Rinpoche, receiving the Padma Bhushan Award the same year. People were coming to our home in droves, and there was no time for my mother to genuinely grieve for her loss even though Bakula Rinpoche was incredibly supportive of her during this period.

Fortunately, she also had a lot of people to lean on, particularly her elder sister, brother, mother, and other relatives.

'They gave me a lot of love, comfort, support, and solace during this incredibly difficult period in my life. But it was your father who was my biggest pillar of support. Besides offering words of comfort and solace, he was always there for me emotionally and physically. He stood by me during this difficult time, and subsequently, when I got pregnant with our second child, he was there for all doctor visits. Even before the birth of my first child, he did the same, but his care, love, and companionship grew even stronger during this period. He took care of all my needs, wants, sat through the difficult times with me, and showed a lot of inner resilience even though he was hurting too,' she said.

My mother also found solace in her faith as a practising Buddhist. Living with Rinpoche, who regularly prayed during her second pregnancy, my mother also found peace in scripture.

'Losing our first child the way we did was heartbreaking. While I was devastated mentally, your mother was deeply hurt, both mentally and physically. So, I had to look out for her. We had been married for a little over a year at the time of losing our baby, and there was nothing else I did but be there for her at all times, comfort her, offer her words of advice and consolation. While we were fortunate to have our family around us during this difficult time, we, first of all, had each other. Through these difficult times, our love grew stronger,' said my father Wangchuk.

Despite the intense tragedy, my parents tried to have another child, and on 22 April 1989, I was born in New Delhi.

As expected, my birth gave them a lot of joy.

'Words can't express the joy that had come into our lives after you were born. Since your birth and twelve years later, your brother Rinchen Namgyal, we have been completely invested in raising both of you. We didn't have time to talk or contemplate our loss in a serious manner. It was all about moving forward, and making the most of what life had given us,' my father adds.

Speaking to my parents' generation, what seems to emerge is a definitive sense of stoicism in the face of untold tragedies. My paternal grandmother lost two children in similar circumstances until she gave birth to my father's youngest siblings, Tshering Namgyal, who is today a serving officer with the Indian Air Force, and a sister Phuntsog Angmo.

'My mother, for example, lost two children before my younger brother was born. But she didn't have time to grieve or consider any sort of remedy for the scars those events had left behind. Living in challenging climatic and economic conditions with no medical facilities or guarantees of where our next meal was going to come from, the objective was survival. She suffered deeply in silence but had the perseverance to move forward with her life. And she is not the only example in a region like Ladakh to show that level of perseverance,' said my father.

It's a stoicism I see in my mother as well. While she found other ways to grieve and bounce back from the tragedy, she is firm on the idea that issues like the loss of a child, stillbirth, miscarriage, or abortions must be talked about more openly.

'Frankly, I hadn't thought about the loss of my first child for the last thirty years. Raising you and your brother became my way of healing from the loss. The sheer happiness at seeing the two of you grow up has given me immense joy,' said my mother.

God knows, my brother and I can vouch for the love she showered upon us.

'But this is not how every mother heals from the loss of a child. We must ensure that we can have these discussions with a lot more openness. The best way to heal any mental scar is to first talk about it. We must open more avenues for it,' she adds.

Lessons learnt

For my father, the loss had shaken him out of his complacency when it came to childbirth.

'Growing up, we assumed that getting married and having a child were just rites of passage that happened rather smoothly. What the death of our first child taught us was that we should never assume things will work out smoothly. The episode gave us a lot of insight into the process and how to avoid these pitfalls. See, back then we weren't made aware of the difficulties and possible complications that come with childbirth. Of course, it didn't help that the doctor we saw at the time didn't pay closer attention to your mother, but more knowledge, awareness, and information wouldn't have gone amiss,' said my father.

There is no question that my parents have tried to pass on the hard lessons they learnt to my other relatives, cousins, and family friends who went onto have children of their own.

My mother, however, has some definitive advice for other prospective mothers.

Her suggestion is to, first of all, ensure the best available doctor attends to their needs. If they can afford it, mothers must never compromise on the quality of doctors. She also suggests that expecting mothers must attend regular check-ups, keep themselves informed with the latest information, ask many questions, seek answers with firmness, and if they feel anything is minutely off they must never hesitate to get themselves checked thoroughly.

'When I was pregnant with my first child, I never really raised any of these doubts with great clarity. Plus, we didn't have the internet, and they never quite discussed these things on TV or popular media. So, I was clueless for the most part. Fortunately, for my second pregnancy, I had Dr Manorama Bhutani at Moolchand Hospital in New Delhi overseeing my care. She ensured that I was kept informed about the child and my health at all times,' recalls my mother.

Talking about this episode with my parents has been a deeply cathartic experience. I had always feared that talking about it may open some old wounds they had bandaged over a long time ago.

Although that feeling of loss was palpable in their voice when I brought it up, what I also heard was a desire to share everything with their son, including their pain.

For that, I will always thank them.

Section V

All It Takes is One Person

'In a gentle way, you can shake the world.'

Mahatma Gandhi

No One Goes Hungry

Vidya Raja

Arup Sengupta carries his oxygen cylinder everywhere he goes. Seven years ago, he was detected with Chronic Obstructive Pulmonary Disease (COPD). But neither illness nor exhaustion stops this seventy-year-old tuberculosis survivor from going to his second home, Notun Jibon—a Kolkata-based NGO he founded to rehabilitate sex workers and their children.

'Notun Jibon means new life and I will continue to serve those in need and give them a chance at a new life until my last breath,' said Arup.

He started his organization four years ago and today it supports and educates more than forty children of sex workers in Kolkata and has been instrumental in saving many women from abusive marriages.

Series of Tragic Events

Arup was born in 1952 in an affluent family. After a few happy years, tragedy struck. The year 1968 left him devastated—he lost his father, his mother turned to alcohol to cope, and his elder sister began working in dance bars to support the family.

As if this was not enough, Arup soon found out that he had tuberculosis.

'In 1968, when my neighbours got wind of my illness, I was thrown out of my locality. I see how COVID-19 patients are shunned today, and it certainly reminds me of that.'

With no family support, he found a roof at a shelter home.

'TB was claiming many lives. I remember all the TB patients would be cooped up in one room where I saw death up close. Every time a machine beeped, we knew we had lost another person.'

However, of the many unfortunate souls in that room, only two survived. One of them was Arup who regained his strength and health after two years of intensive care.

Notun Jibon—A New Life

Arup had lost everything. Yet, he had been given a second chance at life. He did odd jobs to fund his education, such as playing guitar and drums in weddings and other occasions.

After completing his college studies, he worked in the corporate world in the FMCG and human capital management sectors for more than forty-five years across Mumbai, Delhi, and Bengaluru.

Four years ago when the time to retire from his professional life came, Arup chose to settle down in Kolkata. 'I was returning to my home city after twenty years,' he said.

Once there, he saw a changed Kolkata.

'The city I left as a young boy had changed. I came back to poverty, apathy, and a general sense of disillusionment. No one should go to bed at night on a hungry stomach. When I meet my maker I need to have my answers ready and be able to look at him and tell him I did all I could to make a difference,' he said.

On 31 December 2016, with Rs 10,000, Arup stepped out to buy blankets, which he distributed that night. 'With that Notun Jibon was born.' In 2016, he registered the NGO as a Trust. While the primary aim of the organization was to teach underprivileged children, they have now expanded into creating a self-help group for women, especially sex workers.

Working for Underprivileged Women and Kids

The organization employs eight women, referred to as the Nari Shakti team, who are from disadvantaged backgrounds with some being former sex workers.

They manage Notun Jibon and work in various roles such as teachers, managers, and in charge for raising funds. Jhumki Banerjee, secretary of Notun Jibon, said, 'Arup *da* rescued me from an abusive marriage. I have known him for a little more than four years now. He is constantly working.' Jhumki looks after all the fieldwork and is also a trustee with the organization.

Arup is blown away by the Nari Shakti team for the strength they have and the kind of work they do with the children and their rescued sisters. 'Knowing that even after my death, the organization will march forward in their able hands is very satisfying,' he said.

Besides these women, there are nine men who work with the organization on a voluntary basis.

To concentrate on the children of the rescued sex workers, Arup started Sahaj Path, a sub-unit of Notun Jibon. The children aged between three and twelve come every evening for classes and are given a mug of milk and a banana each. The volunteers then impart basic education to these kids—reading, writing, and numeracy.

Work During the Pandemic

The organization provides a weekly ration package consisting of three kilos of rice, two kilos of potato, half a kilo of dal, and mustard oil to children who are not able to come to attend classes. Every morning Arup, Jhumki, and another volunteer from the organization set off in a car filled with ration and masks. 'While life goes on in the villages despite the COVID-19 pandemic, it is ration and food that is scarce. We are filling that void,' he said. He has also ensured that the volunteers and members of the NGO got full salaries during this lockdown period.

So far, Notun Jibon has provided ration to almost 400 sex workers. 'Arup da is not one to care about where his next meal will come from,' Jhumki said, 'If he has Rs 20 in his wallet, he will keep Rs 5 to help him return home and give away everything else.'

And What about Funding?

'I have managed to gather many well-wishers over the years. One post on social media and I see my friends coming forward to graciously support me. All my savings of forty-five years have gone into this organization. I still have a few years of life left in me—and until then I must go on.'

*Arup Sengupta passed away in May 2021.

The Hospital Hut

Jovita Aranha

In 1992, doctor-couple Regi M. George and Lalitha visited Sittilingi. Tucked near the foothills of the Kalrayan and Sitteri hill ranges, this remote tribal village in Dharmapuri district, Tamil Nadu, was cut off from the rest of the modern world.

It was home to 'Malavasis' or 'Hill People' who eke out a living through rain-fed agriculture.

How did the couple get there?

The couple first met as students of the Government T.D. Medical College, Alappuzha. In the early 1990s, after completing their medical training, Dr Regi and Dr Lalitha worked in a hospital in Gandhigram. People from far-flung areas travelled miles for the treatment of preventable illnesses such as diarrhea and childhood pneumonia.

Rattled by the lack of healthcare access, the couple decided to backpack for a year, and document the most sensitive areas in need of help. This quest led them to Sittilingi. What disconcerted them most was the sheer lack of healthcare facilities. In the advent of any medical emergency, the tribals would have to travel to Salem or to Dharmapuri. Because the nearest hospital was more than fifty kilometres away and to find one in the event of surgical intervention meant travel over 100 kilometres!

What pushed the couple further was that this hamlet recorded an infant mortality rate of 150 per 1000 babies, the highest in all of India! One out of five babies in the Sittilingi Valley died before their first year, and many mothers died during childbirth. Located in the middle of a forest, buses ran four times a day. But getting to the bus stand required a long walk, lasting several hours. It could have been easy for Regi and Lalitha to walk away. But they didn't.

They decided to stay and make affordable healthcare available to Sittilingi's two lakh people. Since then, it's been twenty-five years and the couple is only moving forward with their project, Tribal Health Initiative (THI).

The hospital was functioning from a hut that had a single room which operated as an out-patient and in-patient unit. All it had was a 100-W bulb and a bench for the patient to lay on. Dr Regi said, 'We had no money to buy land, so we set up a small clinic on government land, nothing more than a small hut built by the tribals. We worked out of this hut for three years, conducting deliveries and minor surgeries on the floor.'

Friends and well-wishers donated funds to build a ten-bedded hospital. Today, they have come a long way from the thatched hut to a thirty-five-bed full-fledged hospital, which is equipped with an ICU and ventilator, a dental clinic, a labour room, a neonatal room, an emergency room, a fully functional laboratory, a modern operation theatre, and other facilities such as X-Ray, ultrasound, endoscopy, and echocardiography, like any other modern hospital. Besides, the infant mortality rate in Sittilingi has reduced to 20 per 1000, now one of the lowest in India. Moreover, no mothers have died in childbirth in the last ten years!

How did the couple achieve it?

Most deliveries in these areas happened at home. A lack of knowledge about childbirth complications or adequate postnatal care led to a very high rate of infant and maternal mortality.

He shared, 'We started training health auxiliaries who were tribal women in their 40s and 50s to identify complications during childbirth. They visited homes in their respective areas during each delivery and ensured hygiene and sanitation. For instance, they checked if the umbilical cord was cut and tied properly.' He adds that in the case of a complicated pregnancy, they would ensure that the mother was rushed to the hospital as soon as she went into labour. These women also visited the new-born within a week to check upon its health.

When they first began, they had to raise funds, even for the simplest procedures. They were also isolated without family or friends.

Besides, their two boys were young and had no schools in the vicinity. But they did not give up. The boys were home-schooled until class four.

Was there resistance among the tribals? Naturally.

But over the years, looking at their work and hardships, all to give the community the best healthcare, helped the community trust the couple.

'They had not seen a real doctor in a long time. If a child were admitted due to meningitis, the villagers would think it was affected by spirits and look for a witch doctor. In the case of snakebite, they wanted to do a puja. We learnt that one of the most important practices was never to counter their beliefs. If they said they wanted a puja to be conducted, we let them do it by the bedside.'

Dr Regi adds how their idea was to make quality healthcare available and affordable. Even today, deliveries are conducted at costs as low as Rs 1000, and 80–90 per cent of OPD admissions are reserved for the tribal population. 'Some may think it is biased, but it is really them (the tribals) who need our help the most,' he insists.

How then does the hospital run?

Sustenance is difficult, but the couple isn't giving up.

'We charge nominal amounts. In most cases, people pay, but there are times when they just give us what they have. So the hospital's annual turnover, donations from good Samaritans, mostly Indians and NRIs and CSR funds, help us run THI without any government help.'

Are they in need of funds? Yes. But not for expansion but to further subsidize treatments for the poor.

'We do not want cost to hinder their access to healthcare. So, whether they can afford it or not, we want to help them. And of course, there is a constant need for money to keep these services running. We issue a pink card for all the babies born in the hospital, which allows them free care until the age of three. Because this service is free, parents take their children to the hospital. But if this service were to stop because of the lack of funds, the parents won't get their children to the hospital until their health deteriorates drastically,' he informed.

Similarly, they also run an old-age insurance scheme which provides access to free healthcare all-year round at Rs 100.

But their work doesn't end here. The couple has also started an array of other projects to empower the community.

Employing Women

More than 95 per cent of their staff is tribals. Dr Lalitha has been ensuring that women employed at THI also get employee benefits such as Provident Fund (PF) and gratuity.

'Most of our nurses, lab technicians, paramedics, and health auxiliaries are tribal boys and girls, who have been trained by us or others. It is a hospital for the tribals by the tribals, operating in a fifty-kilometers radius, serving one lakh people every year.' Getting women on board wasn't easy. Especially when it was uncommon for daughters to work since they were married off early. Today, these women are skilled to the extent that they can run the hospital without supervision.

Organic Farming

Under Sittinlingi Organic Farmers' Association (SOFA), formed in 2004, they have mobilized over 500 farmers to give up the use of pesticides and grow chemical-free food, providing a green solution to long-standing woes of low yield, uncertain incomes, and infertile land.

The couple is also preserving the history and cultural heritage of the tribe by reviving the dying art of Lambadi embroidery. This art form is an amalgamation of pattern darning, mirror work, cross stitch, overlaid and quilting stitches with borders of 'Kangura' patchwork done on loosely-woven dark blue or red handloom base fabric.

Often mistaken as Kutchi (Kachhi) embroidery because of mirror work, the shells and coins are unique to this type of embroidery, with the stitches being different.

Dr Lalitha is working towards promoting the Lambadi handcrafts under the name 'Porgai', which stands for 'pride' in the Lambadi dialect.

Under the brand 'Svad', women entrepreneurs are given credits to make organic products using local produce. They make over twenty-five organic products which includes powders of different grains, millets, and spices, helping them earn additional income.

Insurance

They also launched a farmer insurance policy, under which every farmer family is insured for Rs 50,000 in case of death. This money is pooled from within the community, where every farmer contributes Rs 100.

Dr Regi observes, 'Just building and running a hospital isn't enough. Whether it is eating healthy chemical-free food by adopting organic farming or promoting entrepreneurship among women, the key to a healthy community is dependent on upliftment in different fields.'

In his final message to other healthcare experts, Dr Regi says, 'Our minds were full of doubts when we started. We had no money when we started, but we had sincerity of purpose. And sometimes, you just have to close your eyes, trust yourself and take that leap of faith. Like Paulo Coelho says, "When you want something, all the universe conspires in helping you to achieve it." The same happened to us. There is a crying need in our country, and we need to extend a helping hand.'

Shillong's 'Dr Dre'

Rinchen Norbu Wangchuk

Lamonte Pakyntein, a thirty-year-old Hip Hop and R&B producer from Shillong popularly known as D-Mon, is the man behind the music that preserved my sanity during the COVID-19 pandemic. Growing weary of self-isolation and sending condolence messages to friends who had lost their loved ones on a near daily basis, I was fortunate enough to find D-Mon's music marked by beautiful chord progressions, soulful melodies, and messages of resilience.

The song 'Don't Stop', featuring his bandmates Big-Ri (Ritik Roy Malngiang) and D-Bok (Donbok Kharkongor) from the Khasi Bloodz, who stand at the vanguard of Shillong's Hip Hop movement, and the supremely talented Meba Ofilia, begins with these words of fortitude:

> *Here's to the heartaches that pulled you through.*
> *Here's to the walls you built to stop them coming back to you.*
> *Here's to the bad times you've been there before.*
> *And oh your feet are sore and you can't do it anymore.*
> *Don't stop, keep going, and don't stop.*
> *Don't stop, it's working, don't stop.*

D-Mon composed it at a time when he contemplated giving up music altogether. Like most struggling independent artists around the world, his music wasn't paying the bills. Not coming from privilege, he didn't know whether he could continue pursuing his life's passion.

'Like many independent artists, that feeling of giving up has always lingered in my mind. But it's the sheer passion for our craft that drives us. When the final product is done, it automatically becomes worth it,' said D-Mon.

Cutting a long story short, he found a way, and more than a year later released 'Done Talking' featuring Big-Ri and Meba Ofilia, who won the Best India Act at the 2018 MTV Europe Music Awards. In the same year, he managed to save enough money to finish constructing the studio for his label Mix & Flow Productions, which ranks among the best in the North-east today.

Sounds of Shillong

Born on 17 December 1990 in Shillong, D-Mon was raised by his grandparents as his mother, a government servant, worked in Kolkata. Struggling with epilepsy in school, he was surprisingly not very fond of music early on, although it was all around him.

'At a very early age, my uncles made me listen to a lot of rock music. On Sundays, my grandparents would play gospel music, which had a massive influence on me, for the whole household. In fact, the first time I ever performed in front of an audience was during a Sunday school church service. Folk music was introduced to me through the radio every morning before school. I consumed it like it was a part of my breakfast. Also, many members of my family played various instruments—grandma played the piano, my grand uncle played the accordion, and my uncle played the guitar. One way or another, all these elements played a role in helping me develop a love for music,' said D-Mon.

His ear for music came from listening to international artists such as Bon Jovi, Scorpion, Steely Dan, Jimmy Reeves, and Robert Cray, while there were local inspirations from Shillong as well which include R. Waroh Pde, Donbor Rynjah, and Amio Lyngshkor.

Hip Hop, however, found its way to D-Mon later on in high school, listening to albums from the 1990s such as Tupac Shakur's 'All Eyez On Me', Warren G's 'Take a Look Over Your Shoulder', 'Ready to Die' by The Notorious B.I.G., and Dr Dre's 'The Chronic'. He would play these albums on his uncle's cassette player in his room or outdoors with his friends.

'I started writing rap verses around 2004. It's a funny story because I started writing raps as a way to remember my answers back in elementary school. So, I would rhyme stuff such as important historic dates and significant names, and it would work. As I grew older, I started to realize I had a knack for writing and it gradually turned into crafting verses. In the beginning, I struggled a lot but as time progressed and with practice, I got better,' he recalled.

Khasi Bloodz

It was during high school at a neighbourhood cybercafé where he met Big-Ri through a mutual friend JCK (Jason Kharchandy). Bonded by their love for Hip Hop, the three of them would meet at the internet café, which became their default hang-out spot.

'D-Bok, on the other hand, came to one of our school concerts in which I was performing a rap song, which I dedicated to Tupac Shakur and The Notorious B.I.G. There was a mutual love we shared for those artists, which led to our friendship. D-Bok then began joining the three of us at the cybercafé regularly. It started with us listening to some rap music at the cafe which then turned into us rapping over beats. After rapping popular songs for a while, we realized the potential within us to write our own verses and began working on our craft. On 19 September 2009, which is Big-Ri's birthday, we formed the Khasi Bloodz. He came up with the name,' said D-Mon.

One of the first songs they wrote was 'Rising Stars' in 2009. However, they only officially released the song in 2013 because they felt that the quality of production wasn't up to scratch. 'We wanted better quality on the production. So, we took time and earned some money, which we could pay to record our song at a professional studio,' he added.

Each member found their way of earning some money on the side as they began studying in college. For instance, D-Mon would paint houses after exams, sell posters, and work at his uncle's coffee shop and a friend's restaurant during his free time. All their side hustle, however, wasn't enough to pay for a recording session at a professional studio.

'So, I dropped out of college to find more ways of reaching my goal, which my family wasn't happy about. But I soon had the good fortune of meeting Mr Bari Khonglah, who was a renowned sound engineer back in the day. He ran a studio called Basement Studio, and I sought a chance to work for him in exchange for some studio time. I would help out with carrying speakers for outdoor events. And instead of paying us a salary, he provided us with the opportunity to record our songs and helped us mix and master them,' said D-Mon.

Released in 2013, the song and the official video for it put them on the map. Even though Hip Hop had always been around in Shillong, there weren't any artists truly representing the city and Khasi identity in this particular space quite like the members of the Khasi Bloodz. 'Khasi Bloodz was officially the first artist/group to represent it for the town. It's one of the biggest honours that we hold dearly to this day,' he said.

But the hustle never stopped. Even as late as 2017–18, D-Mon and D-Bok were making sandwiches and burgers and selling them to offices, cafés, and canteens in the city. The money they made was spent on buying instruments, recording equipment, etc. In many ways, the Khasi Bloodz exemplified the do-it-yourself (DIY) ethic of Hip Hop. Starting out in 2009, there were six members in the group. Today, however, it's just D-Bok and Big-Ri.

Shillong's Dr Dre

Beyond writing verses, D-Mon realized that he had an ear for music when he made the beat for 'Rising Stars'. He stumbled onto a trumpet-like sound on the Yamaha DGX-500 keyboard, which ended up being the melody for the song, following which the drums and the rest were added.

As the Khasi Bloodz began to make their mark, not just in Shillong but the entire Northeast and beyond, D-Mon came together with his best friend and sound engineer, Ardon Samuel Rumnong, to launch their label Mix & Flow

Productions in 2016. As he continued to make music and perform for audiences, the next two years were also spent constructing the studio.

'The total cost for setting up the studio was approximately Rs 10 lakh. To get here, it took years of saving, building, and investing. I can't forget to mention the incredible role my grandparents played during this journey. The main drive behind setting up a studio was to primarily help and provide opportunities for untapped talent in Shillong. As soon as the studio was established, I was able to put all my focus into music,' he said.

As a producer, he has worked closely with and given a platform to young talents from Shillong like singer/rapper/songwriter Meba Ofilia, Reble (Daiaphi Lamare), Dappest (Dapher U-Na-Ki Laloo), while collaborating with other talent from the North-east.

He adds, 'Ever since I knew I had an ear for production, I fell in love with the art form. By 2018, I had fully transitioned to production. Big-Ri and D-Bok were always supportive and knew that one day I would make this transition. Today, while I produce for other artists, revenue for the studio comes in through clientele appointments and other musical projects.'

Vikramjit Sen (a.k.a Feyago), an indie rapper and producer based out of Kolkata, said, 'D-Mon is my favourite producer from the North-east—the "Dr Dre of Shillong". He's a perfectionist, who does not compromise on his craft or artistic integrity. His music is an acquired taste unlike say Stunnah Beatz (Rajdeep Sinha), a popular Guwahati-based producer, who delivers guaranteed hits. But if you want to break the boundaries of your artistry as a rapper or an R & B singer, D-Mon is the man for you. His work is as good as some of the most soulful jazz, blues, or rock music that have come out of India. In order to enter his studio, you have to be all about the music. As a rapper, you're not going to get away with tone-deaf bars.'

'D-Mon is usually fun and laid back, but his music has to be perfect. I've learnt a lot working with him. He is honest when it comes to telling me what's good and what's not,' said Reble.

Feyago adds, 'If I were to make a food analogy, his work is like caviar, which is also an acquired taste. You may not enjoy his songs in the first few seconds and pop open some champagne. His music is more like sipping a glass of fine wine with a book in your hand.'

What also makes him stand out is his emphasis on using live instruments. 'I was always fond of live instruments like drums, keys, bass, guitars, etc. The natural and organic sound that a real instrument brings to the table is important to me. My production style is a merging of two genres like Hip Hop and R&B, mixing old sounds and new and bringing my signature. I have taken inspiration from acclaimed producers like Jimmy Iovine and Hans Zimmer,' explains D-Mon.

'His approach to production follows the mantra that analogue is the meat, and digital is the gravy. Beat production is music, but it's a little different from musicality. If you drop a hard 808 beat, put hi-hats on it and rap, you may impress the Hip Hop crowd. But D-Mon makes music for people who have never listened to Hip Hop before or aren't into it. Compared to most Hip Hop producers, he makes music, not just beats. There is a key difference between a beatmaker and a musical composer. D-Mon is an outright composer who happens to be into Hip Hop. I can count the number of

Hip Hop producers in India who do this on one hand,' observes Feyago.

Even though Hip Hop artists and producers around India are racking up hits and massive online views, D-Mon doesn't feel the pressure to fit in. 'Fitting in doesn't concern me because I've always been focused on working on my own sound. The aim has always been to support young talent who haven't been discovered yet. That's what drives me.'

'D-Mon is always on the lookout for new talent and wants to give them a platform. He has been one of the biggest factors in pushing the Hip Hop–R&B scene to its glory in Shillong and the North-east since his time with the Khasi Bloodz. Today, he provides young artists with immense support to carry out their art,' said Reble.

While the pandemic has proven to be a struggle for his label, spirits remain high. Suffice to say, D-Mon transmitted that spirit to listeners like me who grew weary of the pandemic. 'I don't know what the future holds for us but I'm positive that we'll keep putting in the effort "2 Produce And Create" quality music,' he said.

His Quest for Healing

Serene Sarah Zachariah

For the past nineteen years, fifty-five-year-old Dr Vincent Xavier has been travelling into the dense forests of southern India to look after the sick and ailing in tribal communities. The conscientious doctor walks on foot to reach inaccessible areas, carrying basic medical equipment himself.

Treading into territories where several other doctors have refused to serve because of fear of wild animals, Dr Vincent, who is lovingly called the 'Makka Doctor', has been a support system for the tribal community in Seethathod, Kerala, saving many lives with his timely service over two decades.

How the 'Makka Doctor' Won Many Hearts

After graduating from the Tirunelveli Medical College in 1995, Dr Vincent moved back to his home in Nagercoil and served at the Mission Hospital there for six years.

'Those were the first few years of my career and it was also when I got married and started a family. My wife was from Thiruvananthapuram, Kerala, and it was during one of my visits to her place that I heard about Seethathodu village in Pathanamthitta, Kerala. She explained how the tribals in the area were not getting proper medical assistance since it was a remote area. Several doctors who were appointed to the primary health centre in the village refused to go because of the wild elephants and tigers. When I heard this, I immediately decided to take up the job,' Dr Vincent explains.

Though he charges regular rates for the services rendered, he does not take money from underprivileged families.

So in 2001, Dr Vincent started visiting these tribal communities twice a week. With limited roads and no access to public transport to these dense forests, he began travelling on foot.

'Although the villagers in Seethathod warned me that the forest areas were risky because of the wild animals, I decided to go ahead. From thermometers to a pressure gauge, I carry most of the basic equipment that was required,' he said.

'The first year was difficult because I had to establish a relationship with the tribals and earn their trust. For them, I was an outsider and they needed time to understand my purpose. But in just two years, they began treating me as their own and started calling me the "Makka doctor",' Vincent explains.

'Makka means "children" in their tribal dialect so Makka doctor roughly translates to children's doctor. That was the kind of relationship I shared with them. They saw me as a fatherly figure and would even call me to their homes during my weekly visits,' he adds.

Braving Dense Forests, Animals to Save Lives

Dr Vincent's wife, Mini, who has been his huge support throughout his journey, has seen several instances in her husband's life where he has gone out of his way to help the tribals.

'In 2010, there was an eighteen-year-old tribal girl who was pregnant and was due to deliver in a couple of weeks. Vincent was not expecting the baby for another week, so he had planned his visits accordingly. But at 2 a.m. we received a phone call from the villagers who told us that the young girl went into labour and was bleeding severely. It was really dark at night and there was absolutely no way to reach there in time, but Vincent was determined to save this girl's life,' Mini remembers.

'He grabbed all the medical equipment he needed and left. The villagers had already called an ambulance from the nearest hospital in Vandiperiyar to Seethathod. But even before the ambulance reached, Vincent was able to reach and give her the primary care she needed. Both the mother and the baby were saved that day,' she adds.

'The child is ten years old now and the family calls me home every year for his birthday. And it's instances like these that have given me a sense of purpose,' said Dr Vincent.

Mannan, twenty-four, one of the tribals from the village was also saved by Dr Vincent's timely treatment.

'When I was just sixteen, I was bitten by a viper on my way home. Although this wasn't a rare incident in our area, I did not have anyone nearby to help me out and the situation had worsened by the time the villagers had arrived. But thankfully,

Dr Vincent was on his visit that day and instantly put me on fluids at the primary health centre,' Mannan explains.

'Besides being a doctor, on every visit, he brings his own ration kits and other food items for struggling families,' Mannan adds.

By 2009, Vincent's wife moved back to Nagercoil from Trivandrum, while Vincent decided to stay back and rent a house in Seethathod. 'Although there were several opportunities back home, I couldn't let the community down. So ever since 2009, I've been staying in Seethathodu twice every week. But with the pandemic, I have been staying here for more than three months now,' Vincent said.

'Although I was supposed to retire this year, the government has extended the retirement age to sixty. And even if I do retire, I will always be the "Makka doctor" for these tribals and that makes me content,' he concludes.

Left Blind, She Now Helps Others

Divya Sethu

A teacher, a counsellor, Uttarakhand's ambassador for women empowerment, and an acid attack survivor—Kavita Bisht has many labels to go by. But the foremost is that of a young, jovial girl, who had hopes, dreams, and her entire life ahead of her.

'My childhood in Ranikhet was full of joy and an abundance of freedom,' Kavita said. 'My family never put any restrictions on me in terms of where I should go, who I should talk to, or what I should be doing. I was always interested in social work, so I spent most of my time doing that. I spent my childhood learning art, painting, and sewing. I was also very mischievous.'

Kavita lived with her parents, brother, and two sisters. Her elder sister died when she was twenty-one years old due to a kidney infection in 2007. This affected her father severely, and the family began suffering because he was often unable to go to work due to the trauma. To earn additional income, Kavita moved to Noida, Uttar Pradesh, in 2007.

A Twist of Fate

'After high school, I went to Noida to work. A man, who used to live a few gullies down from where I stayed, wanted to befriend me. I think he would see me come and go to office, but I'd never seen him, and didn't even know who he was. My friend's brother used to live in the same area as him, and he managed to find my number through his contact. The messages started coming around November or December, and they'd all entail him asking me to [at first] be his friend, and later to marry him. He also sent me a present for Christmas. I was not interested, and turned him down repeatedly,' said Kavita.

She would later find out that this man had warned her friend in January that Kavita seems to be 'too proud of how beautiful she is', and that if she wouldn't marry him, he wouldn't let her be with anyone else. But Kavita was never informed of his clear threat that he would disfigure her somehow, and when she heard, it was already too late. 'I'm not sure why she didn't tell me. Maybe she didn't believe it herself,' she said.

On 2 February 2008, Kavita was at the bus stop early in the morning. 'I remember the time very clearly—5:15 a.m. Two men with their faces covered came on a bike, and one threw acid on me,' she said. 'I'd just turned 19 only two months before.'

Till at least 2–2:30 p.m. that day, no hospital admitted her. They all demanded she be accompanied by a guardian, and file an FIR before she could be admitted. At the police station, too, they demanded a guardian accompany her. 'I, along with a few people who had come to help me, took several rounds of

Noida that day,' she said with a grim chuckle. 'When I failed to report to work that day, my manager called my landlord. The company eventually found out I'd been attacked, and they finally sent an ambulance to come get me. I was taken to Safdarjung Hospital in Delhi at around 3:30 p.m.'

Coming to a Standstill

For six days, Kavita remained unconscious. 'When I finally regained consciousness, I couldn't even open my eyes. My parents had come a few days before, and they initially weren't told that I'd been attacked with acid. They just thought I'd been in some sort of an accident,' she said. Kavita underwent treatment for months, with doctors attempting to salvage as much of her face as they could. Throughout, she slipped in and out of consciousness, and her eyesight remained a concern for doctors. A year later, she was told she'd never regain her vision.

The man was caught and arrested, but this would not be the end of her woes. 'While I was unconscious in the ICU, the man's family threatened mine, and asked us to take the case back. They even threatened my younger sister,' Kavita said. The man was later given bail. She credits her company as having saved her life. 'They paid for my expenses. I might not even be alive today if they hadn't,' she said. After the attack, Kavita returned to her village. 'I remained locked inside my room for two years. If I heard footsteps, I'd be terrified. If I heard a man's voice on the television, I'd be terrified. Sometimes, even hearing my brother or father's voice would scare me. I'd jump every time I heard the noise of a bike,' she said.

She further added, 'People in my neighborhood were vicious. They'd scare my parents by telling them that now that your daughter is blind, no one will marry her. "How will you spend your entire life caring for her? She's a burden to you now", they'd tell them. My parents, who had been trying to remain positive and offer their unconditional support to me, were also dragged down by the things they had to hear daily.' The trauma she was dealing with led her to try taking her own life a few times. 'I didn't have anyone to tell me better,' she says.

A Beacon of Hope

Two years later, Kavita received a letter from the Drishtiheen Training School for the Blind. At first, she refused. But her sister and mother encouraged her to take small steps forward. So Kavita went to the school but didn't find herself fully immersed in what was being taught to her. 'At that time, I thought it was only me who had to live with being blind. I was very dejected. But the centre counselled me, and told me that even the visually impaired can lead a life of happiness. I met many people who had similar stories,' she said.

Later, Kavita took admission in the National Institute of Visually Handicapped in Dehradun. She underwent training in using computers, writing shorthand, and making candles and envelopes. Once her training was complete in 2012, she returned to Haldwani. At a medical camp held by a US-returned doctor, she was encouraged by one of the organizers to move out of her village and aim higher.

Around the same time, she lost her younger sister as well, and this put an additional strain on the family. Her father, who had taken time off to care for Kavita after her attack, lost his job as well. He would remain unemployed for around seven or eight years. Those days, Kavita would have Rs 100 or so to travel to Dehradun from Haldwani and back via bus, and would remain hungry and thirsty most of the time.

She was later employed in the Nirbhaya cell in the district in 2014. From here, things started looking up. With help from government officials, Kavita was recognized for her ongoing social work of counselling and training women in arts and crafts, and awarded around eighteen awards, including the Uttarakhand Rajya Mahila Puraskar, and was declared as Uttarakhand's ambassador for women empowerment in 2015. In 2016, she became the state icon for Uttarakhand, and in Gujarat, was awarded under the Beti Bachao Beti Padhao programme.

In 2017, Kavita was acquainted with Sandeep Rawat, who runs U.S.R. Indu Samiti School in Ramnagar, Nainital, which caters to children with various disabilities. Here, she teaches them basic literacy and numeracy skills. She said, 'Some of these children can't see, some can't hear, some can't walk, and some can't talk. I see them and sometimes feel grateful for where I am. Maybe I don't have my vision, but I have many other things.' The school houses around 82 children, who all love Kavita. 'I just want to see them prosper and grow,' she added.

During the COVID-19 lockdown, Sandeep started a centre for women in need, and named it Kavita Women Support Home. She divides her time between the two, and offers counselling and basic training to the women in the home. Many of these women are senior citizens, who are taught how to make decorations for festivals, and other such creations. 'We teach them craft and sewing, and then help them sell the products.'

'What I find lacking is government support. My compensation stopped when the government changed. They never reached out to survivors, even during the lockdown, to ask how they were doing. I believe even in society at large, survivors who have lost everything are not cared for. We know there have been movies made on acid attack survivors, but I didn't think it showed the full severity of the situation. So many of us survivors have lost our ears, eyes, noses, mouths, and limbs. I feel as if we are sidelined,' she said.

She adds, 'Receiving all the awards was an honour, but it does get hard to remain positive all the time,' she admitted. 'I only remind myself that this must have happened to me for a reason. If life had gone another way, I might have been married off and living with two kids right now. But today, I am an independent woman, who can provide for my family and is helping empower women and children who come from tough backgrounds. This keeps me going.'

Section VI

Business With a Heart

*'Businesses need to go beyond the interests of
their companies to the communities they serve.'*

Ratan Tata

From Banking to Farming

Manabi Katoch

'Our biggest achievements are when customers say they feel healthier, and when our farmers say they can now give a better life to their children, and our eight-year-old daughter said that she wants to become a farmer, just like her Mamma–Papa,' said Prateeksha Sharma with a big smile.

These achievements are all thanks to 'Green and Grains', a 'Farm-to-Fork' business model in which partner farmers are trained to manage production on their land, and their organic produce is delivered to customers' doorstep.

However, the journey was not easy for the banker-turned-farmer couple, Prateeksha and Prateek Sharma.

Seeds of Goodwill

It all began in 1983 in a small village called Dolariya in the Hoshangabad district of Madhya Pradesh. Prateek's father, Praveen Sharma, a postgraduate in English, somehow collected foreign literature on modern farming methods for years, and began selling farming equipment.

Praveen always pushed for the development of the farming community as a whole during his dealings, and that's where the seed of 'collective good' was sown in Prateek's mind. 'I still have the books on Australian and European farming methods gathered by my father. I don't know how he managed to get these staying in a remote village,' said Prateek.

The Rat Race

Things changed in 2003 when Prateek lost his father. Prateek had just graduated at the time, and instead of continuing his father's business, he decided to pursue an MBA and take up a job in the banking sector.

Prateeksha, on the other hand, is an IAS officer's daughter and always wanted to make a difference in others' lives. But farming was never on her mind. 'Being from a service class family, I always thought farming was not the job of the educated, just like most people in cities think,' said Prateeksha.

But a spark for social service remained in them both, buried under their ever-growing banking career at Kotak Mahindra. This spark burst into a flame when their daughter Mihika was born. They researched good food habits and realized how difficult it was to find the right food in a world where chemically enhanced farming is the norm. The search took Prateek back to his village. The couple took a transfer to Bhopal, and Prateek became a weekend farmer in his village, where he built a polyhouse.

'Yes, it was tiring. I was looking after four states then and had to travel for my job frequently. Still, I would drive down to my village every weekend and work on my farm,' said Prateek.

Every Mistake is a Lesson

Building a polyhouse, using all their savings, was their biggest mistake, according to this couple. The first year was a disaster. But it also made them understand the major issues of farmers.

1. A communication gap between policymakers and farmers who did not speak the same language.
2. An expensive cycle of buying seeds, fertilizers, and pesticides to make chemically enhanced farming work.
3. No hold over the marketing of their own produce.

Prateek believed he could overcome the first issue by becoming the farmers' voice to the authorities. He dealt with the second one by farming organically and gathering as much knowledge about it as he could. To do this, he began by visiting and learning from the best organic farmers in the country. He also started learning the science behind farming. He quickly realized that there wasn't a standard method that worked for every farm, soil, and farmer. So Prateek eventually came up with his own methods to fit his surroundings.

'Marketing' could only be tackled if Prateek could completely ditch middlemen, remove the dependency on *mandis* (rural markets), and build a farm-to-fork system.

This was not possible for a single farmer. Hence, in 2015, apart from growing vegetables on his own 5.5-acre organic farm, he partnered with an FPO, the Kalpavalli Greens Producer Company Ltd, with twelve more farmers. By 2016, Prateek had learned enough to quit his job and become a full-time farmer. However, Prateeksha kept working as a banker to support him financially.

Prateek now began to guide farmers on how to develop their soil, what to grow, and when to grow. Then, he would pick up the produce from the farms, get them to Bhopal, grade, clean and pack them, and deliver them to the customers' doorsteps in his car. Initially, he had a few customers in his own building society and Prateeksha's parents' building society. But word spread, and Prateek was soon a 'family farmer' to fifty families.

But delivering only veggies was not enough. There were at least 50 items that a family needed, and the model would become successful only if the basket had all of these. But for this, bigger infrastructure and capital was required. The couple had no idea where they would get that.

The Turning Point

'Quitting my job was not easy. We all know that farming is a totally unglamorous field, and leaving a lucrative banking career for it was almost seen as madness for many. But our corporate friends always supported us. They would tell us how they are proud of us for doing something they wish to do but did not have the courage to do,' said Prateeksha.

One of these friends, Amit Jambulkar, wrote to The Better India about Prateek.

'It was August 2017 when I got a call from Manabi from The Better India. I was thrilled as it was my first media interaction. She asked me for a good time to speak. But I just parked my car then and there and spoke to her for the next 45 minutes,' said Prateek.

The article was read by the Start-up Incubation Centre at IIM Calcutta (IIM Calcutta Innovation Park; IIMCIP), and they contacted Prateek. They went through the selection process, got funding, and this helped them set up their start-up company, Vishalya Foods and Farms Pvt. Ltd. Then, they launched their products under the brand name—Green and Grains.

IIM Calcutta also mentored, trained, helped in capacity building, exposure visits as also the very critical 'Seed Funding' under the INVENT program of the Government of India. Thus, Green and Grains became a registered start-up under the Start-up India program and Start-up Program for the state of Madhya Pradesh.

'Under this program, we were looking for passionate people who could build a sustainable social enterprise. Prateek and Prateeksha's model was a perfect fit for this criteria. The best thing about them was the kind of resilience and dedication they had towards this cause. They were working straight from their heart, which was evident from their customer engagement,' said Gaurav Kapoor, chief business officer, IIM Calcutta Innovation Park.

Next Level, Next Challenge

With the seed fund from IIM Calcutta, Green and Grains could buy their first truck and a bigger warehouse. The next step was to add all the items needed by a household every week in their basket.

Thus, Prateek gathered more farmers who produced grains, spices and fruits too. In addition, they were personally trained by Green and Grains to grow good quality organic products.

'Living the "start-up life" is like being on a roller-coaster ride. It is emotionally and physically draining at times. But we sailed through our highs and lows with unconditional support from my mom and dad, not only emotionally but in operations as well. For example, mom would make a variety of pickles, sauces, chai masala, garam masala for us, using the surplus stock we had so that there was no wastage and our customers just loved these,' added Prateeksha.

'It is so much more convenient for us farmers. We just have to look after production, which is also supported by Prateek bhai. The rest of the tension is taken by Green and Grains. Before this, we had to take our produce to the mandis ourselves. There was no fixed price and no guarantee of sales. Here, the Green and Grains team comes to our farm to pick up our produce. They give us fixed prices and manage our farm waste too. What else do we need? We can't even think of going back to the old cycle again,' said Rakesh Gour, a farmer from Dharamkundi who has been associated with Green and Grains for the past two years.

This growth allowed Prateeksha decide to quit her job as well. She had gained experience in operations and customer handling from her banking career of ten years. Prateek completely took care of the production, and Prateeksha looked after the post-production part, right from segregation, grading to delivery.

With strong support from their mentor, Gaurav and their loyal customers, they kept going. But by February 2020, they were almost broke due to the high working capital involved in the business. The couple took on the losses themselves and never let the farmers or the customers suffer.

The End or The Beginning?

On 12 February 2020, Prateek put out a post on Facebook that he would start a farm training program. Many thought it was just another side hustle. But this was Prateek's last attempt to save Green and Grains. 'That was the toughest day of our life. This was our last hope. If this did not work, we had no way out other than to quit farming. It was not just about us. We could have gone back to our corporate lives again. But what about the farmers associated with us? We knew their life was getting better, and we could make this difference in so many other lives, only if we had money,' said the couple.

Prateek and Prateeksha may not have made it work. But suddenly, a nationwide lockdown was announced during the first wave of COVID back in March 2020. Green and Grains was exactly the model that was required during the lockdown.

People were more health-conscious, hence preferred organic food. However, they couldn't go out, so they needed doorstep delivery. And everyone was looking for options where there was a minimum contact of people. 'Orders kept coming like crazy. The volume was five times more than usual. So Prateeksha would stay up all night and prepare the orders for us. And I would leave early in the morning to pick up the vegetables from the farms and come back only by 11–11:30 p.m. after delivering all the orders,' said Prateek.

This boost gave them the capital they needed to run the business at this scale. And for the first time, Green and Grains made profits. Last year they raised revenues of Rs 60 Lakh. Prateek deployed this money to build technology that could help them in the long run.

Today, Green and Grain aggregates products from farmers from six states and serves more than 2000 families in Madhya Pradesh. They plan to take it to 20,000 families in the next twelve months. They now serve more than 250 products to their customers through home deliveries.

Soon they are planning to serve exotic fruits and spices from the north-eastern states of India, and they envisage taking Green and Grains pan-India in the next three years. 'This journey was a growth journey not only for Green and Grains but for us as well. We have gone through ups and downs like never before, worked on the field, did home deliveries with no staff during the pandemic, went through the highest to our lowest points in life. But that's what made us who we are today. We are so clear in our life right now,' said Prateek and Prateeksha Sharma.

This Grandma is Truly Great

Vidya Raja

It is not every day that you get the chance to speak with a 100-year-old! 'Stay busy and do not interfere in other's lives,' is the mantra that 1920-born Padmavati (Padmam) Nayar lives by.

Not one to while away her time, she is a passionate designer who continues to hand-paint saris with a keen intellect and sharp brush strokes that belie her age, and gives hope and inspiration to many.

Every day, she sets herself a target to work for three hours, and meticulously completes her task for the day. When asked why, she said, 'I enjoy this, and it gives me a great deal of satisfaction.'

Being Productive with Her Time

Padmam wakes up between 5.30 and 6.30 a.m. every day. While she goes through the morning routine of tea and breakfast, she likes to read the newspaper. 'She will make her way to her work desk by 10.30 a.m. and immerse herself in the world of her paints and brushes until almost past 1.00 p.m.,' informs Lata, her daughter.

Designing a sari is a time-consuming and meticulous process. Padmam is very particular about her work and sets herself exacting standards. She first outlines the design, then fills it with colours. She paints on saris made from a variety of materials. 'But working on tussar silk is slightly more challenging,' she said.

'My daughters and daughters-in-law bring the saris to me, and I paint.'

I ask her if she has kept count of the saris she has painted so far, and she laughs, "No, not at all. But I know it is many, many saris so far. I also paint tablecloths and used to do cross-stitch as well,' she said.

It takes Padmam about a month to complete work on a sari. "The money that she makes is generously spent on her grandkids. She has never kept anything for herself,' said Lata.

She charges about Rs 11,000 for one sari, which includes the cost of the sari, and Rs 3000 for a dupatta.

The memory of her first sale is vividly etched in Padmam's mind. It was the first time in her sixty-plus years of existence that she had earned something.

Being Connected with Her Family

The centenarian has five children—Captain Ramachandran Nayar, Captain (Late) Krishnakumar Nayar, Lata Parvathy, Usha Lekshmi, and Jaigopal—seven grandkids, and four great-grandchildren. She is loved and respected immensely, and that comes through in Padmam's voice as talks about how she's had a good life.

Born in Thrissur's Wadakancherry, Padmam was the ninth of ten children. Her early years were spent in Kerala until she moved to Mumbai in 1945 when she got married to K.K. Nayar who worked at Ford Motors. Together they raised five children, and through it all, Padmam nurtured her love for the art. She would often sew clothes for the children, which included everything from dresses for the girls to kurta–pyjamas for the boys.

'As far back as I can remember, Amma would stitch our clothes and enjoy replicating sewing designs that she would see somewhere. But she truly started following her passion and enjoying it only after she had us all well-settled,' said Lata.

Padmam concurs, 'In the beginning, I painted very little, but my daughter, who is a designer was perhaps instrumental in pushing me a little and making me take it up.' Along with this, Padmam also found encouragement in her daughter-in-law, Dr Shubhageetha, and Vijaylaxmi (Lata's sister-in-law from her husband's side).

It wasn't until she was in her mid-60s that Padmam took up her hobby seriously with the encouragement and support from her family members.

'If at 100 I can earn some money, why not?' she states happily.

Being an Amazing Great-grandmother

Padmam's evenings are reserved for a little television, reading some of the WhatsApp messages her grandkids send her, and a mandatory call that she makes to her daughter every night before she calls it a day.

Lata laughs as she said, 'Every night Amma will send a message to my sister saying: "Call now, Usha." This message is promptly followed up with a call my sister makes every night.'

With a large family that is spread across the world, Padmam is more than adept at using social media platforms to stay connected. She uses WhatsApp to send and receive messages, often makes video calls to her grandkids, and stays in touch with family and friends via email.

To celebrate her 100th birthday, the family had organized an online virtual meet, which Padmam enjoyed a lot.

Being an Inspirational Mother

'She is an independent woman. In all these years that she has stayed with me, not once have I had to "look" after her. Even at 100 she bathes herself, and if given a chance would also make her morning cup of tea,' said Lata.

Padmam has taught her children to be self-dependent. Talking about her parenting philosophy, she said, 'Why should I interfere with how someone else chooses to live their life? I am living mine, and I am happy.'

Her message to all women is that age doesn't matter when you want to do something on your own: 'Stay busy, find something that you love doing, and try not to interfere in the lives of others.'

The Man Who Learnt to Bake Bread

Himanshu Nitnaware

The aroma of freshly baked bread wafting from a modest bakery in Pune never fails to tempt passers-by to stop for a loaf or to try some warm cakes. Tokyo Bakery, as the name suggests, offers probably the softest Japanese bread in the city.

Started by Rahul and Arundhati Deo in 2017, the bakery offers a range of Japanese bread that claim to be chemical-free, 'without any additives or preservatives' and, of course, always fresh from the oven.

Japanese loaf, melon pan, anpan, curry bread, and custard bun are some of the traditional Japanese breads offered at this bakery along with fourteen other variants.

But what's interesting is that neither of the partners has ever been a baker.

After graduating as electronics engineer from Pune, Rahul spent about twenty years in the IT industry. His interest in learning the Japanese language in 1990 had eventually paved the way for him to become a successful baker.

'After graduating, I tried doing a business in the field of electronics. One day, I found people lining up in front of a building I passed by regularly that got me curious. They were queuing up for courses in a foreign language,' Rahul said.

Breaking the Language Barrier

With a desire to learn a language that does not require the use of English letters, Rahul signed up to learn Japanese. 'My interest in the subject grew. Over the engineering years, I had realized using electronic components like chips and other materials often came with Japanese specifications. So I thought it would be a good idea to learn the language of a country that is technologically advanced,' he adds.

After studying Japanese for three years, Rahul bagged a job in Fujitsu, the Japanese IT company in Pune. Given his proficient language skills, the company offered him the opportunity to travel to Japan. Rahul then married and made Japan his home from 1996 until 2008.

'In June 2008, we decided to return to India for good, and I requested for a transfer to our Pune IT development center. But then the economic downturn hit and made the situation worse. That's when I decided to quit and continue working as a consultant with Japanese companies,' Rahul said.

He and his wife Arundhati soon began missing the freshly baked soft bread of Japan. 'There are community bakeries in Japan that are very popular. In India, when people fall ill, doctors often discourage patients from eating bread, but in Japan, the doctors ask patients to stop eating rice and change their diet to include bread. The bread I ate here from the grocery store was stale and pumped with chemicals like emulsifiers, preservatives and stabilizers,' he adds. Holding a permanent resident visa, Rahul decided to explore opportunities in Japan.

'I also thought that I could probably learn to bake bread for my own personal interests too,' he said.

Little did he know that the trip would change his life entirely.

Baking My Bread and Eating It Too

Rahul flew to Japan and also managed to find a job. During one of his meetings with a friend, he was introduced to a seventy-five-year-old woman named Soho Nakano.

'Soho Sensei (teacher in Japanese) is a painter, and she was intrigued by the fact that an Indian visited a traditional painting workshop. During our talks, I expressed interest in learning to bake bread, among other topics of discussion,' Rahul said.

Soho also requested to arrange a cross-cultural study tour of her twenty students in India. 'We all flew together for an India tour in 2014 and everyone complained about the bread they consumed, even in five-star hotels,' Rahul said.

Soho then advised Rahul to learn baking in Japan. 'I agreed, and she arranged a five-day training session with the renowned baker Tsunetaka Kawakami,' Rahul said.

After four months of his newly acquired job in Japan, he quit and returned to India with a will to make the best Japanese bread.

But six months of effort still wasn't enough for Rahul to get the bread right. 'I thought it was the ingredients like water, flour, yeast, and salt which were different here,' he said.

To test his theory, Rahul sent some flour to one of his Japanese friends. 'The bread came out well. The water and yeast were the only determining factors for the soft dough, I assumed,' he said.

Back to Basics

In 2015, frustrated with his failed attempts, Rahul went to Japan determined to get his bread right. 'I reached out to Kawakami and carried Indian ingredients this time. The bread turned out beautifully. Recognizing my passion, the pro-baker offered me a job,' he adds.

Rahul said he was offered a generous salary and was even made to handle the overseas business along with learning baking.

Having always worked in an office environment and following a sedentary lifestyle, Rahul suddenly found himself standing all day, working the dough.

'After a week of taking the job, I started getting negative thoughts. I felt like it was a wrong decision,' Rahul said, adding that he slowly got accustomed to the new environment.

After eight months of learning all the skills and documenting notes with the smallest of details required for baking, he returned in January 2016. 'Despite all attempts, I failed again,' Rahul said.

Arundhati, his wife who earlier worked in Life Insurance Corporation, also tried her hands at getting the dough right. She had taken up some basic bread baking classes while in Japan. 'Rahul shared his notes and techniques about his learnings. We changed methods, experimented, but the bread was not good enough to sell it to customers," Arundhati said.

Inviting the Experts

Arundhati said that her husband even thought of importing the flour to make the bread, but that would be an impractical choice.

Rahul had almost given up on baking good Japanese bread. But another opportunity presented itself.

'Kawakami invited me to Japan for a television shoot for a production company that wanted to film him teaching a foreigner. But I invited the crew and Kawakami to India for the shoot instead,' Arundhati said. Fortunately, the parties agreed, and in October 2016 a place was booked to arrange for the shoot.

Rahul said though the parties decided to visit India, he did not have any equipment. 'I roamed the city to rent an oven, and baking equipment, molds and other bakery items required for the set-up. After getting everything in place a night before the crew's arrival and inviting sixty guests, the four-hour shoot was a success,' the baker said.

'It was unbelievable to see Kawakami baking beautiful bread with Indian ingredients. It seemed like he conjured about fifteen types of bread like a magician straight out of the oven,' Rahul said.

The couple then bought a commercial oven, and with more lessons from Kawakami, they worked for the next quarter, perfecting their bread.

The Rising of the Bread

'In four years, we failed hundreds of times before we started sharing it with friends. Slowly, they started paying us and became our initial customers. Word spread and Japanese expats started buying from us as well. On a good day, we baked 100 loaves of bread for customers,' Rahul said.

By June 2017, the couple had a steady stream of customers but the thought of opening a bakery never occurred to them until Rahul's Soho teacher called him.

'Soho became curious about my progress and called to enquire. My teacher was surprised to know that after years of learning to bake, I did not still own a bakery. She also informed me about her trip with twenty-three students to India,' Rahul said.

Soho told her student that it was her dying wish to see his bakery. 'Soho is a motherly figure to me, and she wanted me to have my professional set-up,' Rahul said.

They had a little less than three months to find the right equipment to scale the products commercially and search for a place before Soho arrived in India.

After much struggle, a friend ended their hunt for commercial space by offering his shop to Rahul in a residential township at Bhugaon, about fifteen kilometres from Pune.

On 11 September 2017, the Deo family with Soho and her Japanese students inaugurated Tokyo Bakery.

The bakery started doing well by earning Rs 1 lakh a month, which helped maintain the business. For the next six months, the couple swept the floors, baked loaves of bread, cleaned the dishes, and sold the products by themselves.

What's Next?

By October 2019, with two well-trained staff from a village in Maharashtra, the team of four moved to Baner to set up in a more commercial area to improve the business. The couple sold bread to Mumbai and Ahmedabad and a few from the Japanese community every fortnight.

All publicity is currently through word of mouth, as the bakery has no website or social media presence.

Arundhati said her experience of taking Indian food cooking classes in Japan helped her to standardize the recipes. 'Breaking down the techniques helped to train the staff. The quality of flour differs in each batch in India and adaptations have to be made accordingly. We have learnt this through experience,' said Arundhati.

Rahul adds that the bread recipe has evolved to suit the Indian palate. 'There is also a notion among Indians that a bakery means cakes. To cater to these demands, we have recently introduced cakes and pastries,' he adds.

The couple plans to train their younger son, Parth, in Japanese pastry-making in the coming year as well. 'He expresses interest in baking and wants to experiment with pastries and is heading in that direction,' Rahul adds, expressing that his ultimate wish is to have a bakery café. 'I imagine having a 1000 sq. feet space where people can sit and enjoy the bread and sandwiches with beverages. I want Arundhati to experiment with new bread and I will focus on marketing.'

Tongawala to Masala King

Gopi Karelia

For those who have just started exploring cooking, the MDH Pav Bhaji Masala packet has become a flavourful crutch for them to lean on.

The image of the ever-smiling bespectacled 'Dadaji' in his iconic red turban and white sherwani on the packet assures them that this masala will add an exquisite aroma, texture, and taste to every dish they make. That is why the colourful packets of MDH masalas have always been a part of our culinary repertoire.

This holds for millions across India as it continues to transcend languages, generations, and communities.

MDH, short for 'Mahashian Di Hatti', was founded a century ago in 1919 by Mahashay Chunni Lal Gulati in undivided India's Sialkot region. Over the years, Gulati tirelessly worked to build his small family business into a multi-crore company that promises just one thing—a perfect blend of fragrant Indian spices in a powdered form.

With sixty-four products, including Meat Masala, Kasoori Methi, Garam Masala, Rajma Masala, Shahi Paneer Masala,

Dal Makhani Masala, Sabzi Masala, this FMCG company clocked a revenue of Rs 924 crore in 2017. They export to over a hundred countries and have eight lakh retail dealers and 1000 wholesalers.

From ferrying passengers to selling mirrors and doing carpentry, Gulati is a self-made crorepati who identified the pulse of the nation early on and made a homemaker's life easy with ready-to-use ground spices.

A Class 5 Dropout's Humble Beginnings

Born in 1923 in Sialkot (Pakistan) to Mahashay Chunnilal and Mata Chanan Devi, Gulati had a simple childhood. Spending time with buffaloes near riverbanks, playing *kushti* (wrestling) in *akharas* (place of practice), helping his father sell milk products and going to school occupied his early days.

Disinterested in studies from the very beginning, Gulati dropped out of school in class five and joined his father in their small business of selling mirrors, followed by soaps. He also branched out to other products such as hardware, cloth, and rice trading. The experience he received as a teenager went on to shape his consumer-centric vision in future.

For a brief period, the father–son duo also opened a spice shop under the name of Mahashian Di Hatti, and was popularly known as 'Deggi Mirch Wale'. However, during Partition, the *Deggi Mirch* family had to leave behind all their belongings and migrate to Delhi overnight.

'On 7 September 1947, I reached a refugee camp in Amritsar with my family. I was twenty-three years old at the time. I left Amritsar with my brother-in-law and came to Delhi to look for work. We felt Amritsar was too close to the border and a riot zone. Having travelled to Delhi several times before, I also knew that it was cheaper than Punjab,' Gulati had told *The Wall Street Journal*.

There he was, a young man with only Rs 1500 in his pocket. He used Rs 650 to buy a tonga and started ferrying people from New Delhi Railway Station to Qutab Road and Karol Bagh to Bara Hindu Rao at merely two annas, said the report. As fate would have it, Gulati wanted to go beyond the hand-to-mouth existence. He was confident of earning more in his spice trading business, something he was already an expert at. So, he sold his tonga and bought a small wooden *khokha* (shop) at Ajmal Khan Road in the Karol Bagh area. The banner of 'Mahashian Di Hatti of Sialkot, Deggi Mirch Wale' was up again.

In the next couple of years, he and his younger brother Sat Pal earned a name by word of mouth and local advertisements. Estimating the market potential of spices in India, the brothers opened more shops in areas like Khari Baoli. They also set up the first modern spice store in Delhi in 1953, 'It was the first modern spice store in Delhi. I went to Bombay thrice to get ideas to plan the interiors,' he recalled to *Hindustan Times*.

What Makes MDH Stand Out

Breaking the age-old norm that masalas can only be pure if made at home at a time when fast consumerism was still alien was certainly challenging.

As the business flourished, Gulati sensed the need to make his masalas stand out from the rest and banked all his energies on developing an advertising campaign. It would have to be vibrant and eye-catching.

They used cardboard packaging with the words 'Hygienic, Full of Flavour and Tasty'. A man with no education degree or marketing teams put his photo on the packet. Interestingly, even today, the packaging remains the same with a few changes.

The philanthropist probably never estimated that a straightforward campaign would get so big that 'Dadaji' with a moustache became a brand one day. The psyche behind featuring himself in the advertisements was to let the customers see who they were buying from and build a special connection with them.

And it worked.

'I remember, how as a kid, my mother would ask me to buy groceries. For the longest time, I would tell the shopkeeper to give "dadaji wala masala". Now, as an adult, I first look at the picture and then the name while purchasing *masalas* in the supermarket,' said Roshni Mehra, a consumer from Chennai.

Meanwhile, Sunil Sharma, a Digital Marketing Executive from Noida, believed 'staying close to the roots' worked like a charm, 'It shows their loyalty and commitment towards what they manufacture. Their respect for their humble beginning and belief in quality is what worked for them.' He also pointed out that Gulati played it safe by relying on himself, as 'Celebrities and controversies go hand-in-hand, and this can severely impact the image of the brand. He placed a bet on himself.'

MDH has remained true to its catchphrase '*Asli Masale Sach Sach*' in all its advertisements as well as its superior and consistent quality. While Gulati adapted the technological advancements, he ensured that the taste and quality of masalas remained the same.

Most of the raw materials are imported from Kerala, Karnataka, and even Afghanistan and Iran to maintain consistency.

Chilli powder, coriander, and blended spices are ground in automatic machines (that can manufacture thirty tonnes daily). MDH manufacturing plants are present in several parts of India, including Delhi, Nagpur, and Amritsar.

They also have quality control laboratories that check the quality standards. All their masalas are detailed-to-perfection with no artificial colours or preservatives.

'I have been an MDH fan for the last twenty years, and I have tried other brand masalas too. Unlike MDH, other masalas shed colours while cooking or when washed. Plus, ingredients like clove, mustard, and curry leaves are already added in MDH-formulated mixture masalas, so I do not have to add them separately,' said Swati Harsora, a homemaker from Mumbai.

Not all companies can manage to stay afloat for almost a century, especially in a country like India, that is booming with products and services each day.

Retaining Flavour and Market Position

For a man who traded in multiple sectors, lived through the trauma of Partition, and experienced severe financial crises, relevance in the market and staying ahead of competitors came naturally. After gaining prominence in India and abroad, most companies would set a higher value for their products, but not this spice giant. It has still not budged away from its core principle of affordable pricing.

'We dictate the prices in the market, as rivals follow us to make their pricing strategy. Since we want to keep our business margin low, it helps the overall category grow due to affordability,' Rajinder Kumar, executive vice-president at MDH, told *The Economic Times*.

That said, MDH has also not shied away from accepting change and coming up with distinct flavours like MDH Chunky Chat, Biryani Masala, Amchoor Powder, Dahivada Masala, MDH Meat Masala, Rava Fry Bharwan Sabzi Masala, and so on.

MDH has also been committed to corporate social responsibility through the Mahashay Chuni Lal Charitable Trust. It has established a 300-bed hospital in West Delhi that treats the underprivileged for free. Further, as per the website, the Trust also runs twenty free schools for kids from economically weaker sections of our society.

What was born from a need to overcome financial strain gradually turned into a massive spice business with fans across the globe. This *swadeshi* (indigenous) brand has penetrated all Indian households over the years and continues to dominate our kitchen shelves.

As for Gulati, his remarkable rags-to-riches story will forever remain etched in our memories.